The information contained herein is published and produced by Life Teen, Inc. The resources and practices are in full accordance with the Roman Catholic Church. The Life Teen® name and associated logos are trademarks registered with the United States Patent and Trademark Office. Use of the Life Teen® trademarks without prior permission is forbidden. Permission may be requested by contacting Life Teen, Inc. at 480-820-7001.

Special thanks to Mark Hart for his writing and coordination of this Life Teen resource and for sharing so much of his love for our family of faith, the Communion of Saints.

Thanks to Sean Garrison for his writing and contributions to the finished work and to Alissa Roberts for the many ways she helped to pull so much information together.

Props and many thanks to all those who contributed content, including: Fr. John (Fr. J.) Gerth, Jason Pastore, Tricia Tembreull, Erin Kleckner, Tobi Wedig, Ryan Rousseau, Matt Taylor, Heather Koerner, Jackie Schabold, Jake Etchevarria, Kent Thomson, Theresa Bey and J.J. Bort.

Thanks to Theresa Ratti for the copy editing and to Lisa Epperson and Katie Orlando for their editing and input. Thanks too to Carlos Weaver and Laura Womack for design and layout.

And last, but certainly not least - thanks to Fr. John Gerth for serving as theological editor and consultant.

TABLE OF CONTENTS

GOD'S DESIRE FOR YOU

A priest once told me that, as a follower of Christ, I was called to be a saint. I attempted to correct the priest explaining, "Father, sainthood is not for me, it is for extraordinary people...folks like Mother Teresa". I had the mistaken notion that sainthood was for the few rather than the many. I was wrong.

Put simply, God's desire for you is everlasting life with Him in heaven. That means that He wants you to live a life worthy of the call (Eph. 4:1). Living a life "worthy of the call" is a life of sainthood.

God desires for you to be so in love with Him and so committed to sharing His truth and His love that you are known as a saint in Heaven. Living that way might even leave you considered a saint in the eyes of the world, like Blessed Mother Teresa of Calcutta; living that way could also get you killed, like the countless martyrs who have gone before us.

Today, right now, you are being called by God to be holy, and so am I. The "call to holiness" is a fact woven throughout Scripture, but it is difficult and often rejected for one of two reasons.

1. We don't know what "holy" really means.
2. We aren't always honest with ourselves.

Holy does not mean perfect. Holy means "set apart". The word "holiness" is a word that turns many people off. Some think it is "self-righteous", others think it means you can't have any fun. Still others think "holiness" is something that isn't realistic in today's society where you're supposed to "look out for number one".

When God calls us to be "holy" it means that He sets us apart, *within* the world.

It doesn't mean that we ignore the world, other people or sin, it means that we realize *how* we are to relate to the world. It means that we realize that this world is not our final destination, but that while we are here we are called to live lives that *set us apart* from the rest. We are ordinary people who are made extraordinary *not* by things we do, but by a Father who claims us and loves us and calls us to live for others.

The reason this call is often ignored, however, is the second reason listed above: we're not always honest with ourselves. Self-awareness is a key to true holiness. True self-awareness stems from our understanding that we are sinners and that darkness (sin) exists in our lives. True saints acknowledge the darkness and they refuse to be mastered by it. Saints are constantly drawn to the light (God).

Most sinners think that they are saints but true saints know that they are sinners. It is a sinners' self-awareness that starts them on the path to God. What allows for sainthood is a sinner's honesty about "where they really are" in relationship to Him.

Take a minute to meditate on this verse from St. John:

"If we say, "We are without sin," we deceive ourselves, and the truth is not in us. If we acknowledge our sins, He is faithful and just and will forgive our sins and cleanse us from every wrongdoing. If we say, "We have not sinned," we make Him a liar, and His word is not in us." - **1 John 1:8-10**

I know that often times I am not completely honest with myself or with God. This verse today convicts me to constantly be *real* and *authentic* with God, acknowledging where my heart and my life are in relationship to Him. Hopefully it does the same for you.

He knows our sin. It's our reaction and response to sin and to darkness, however, that makes the difference to God. Choosing the light of God transforms us from sinners into saints. Choose to live like a saint today and then tomorrow choose to do so, again. You won't always be "successful" but that's okay, God's grace is enough.

As you read and pray through this book we hope you will learn that your sainthood is not only possible, it is desirable.

And as you read through this *Saintbook*, with courage, pray this prayer:

"God, remove from my life this day anything that will keep me from sainthood."

We believe in you!

Be God's,

- Mark Hart (and the rest of the Life Teen Staff)

MARY QUEEN OF SAINTS

Some people are confused about the Blessed Virgin Mary. They can't seem to figure out "what the big deal" is with her. At times you might be questioned, as a Catholic, as to what exactly the Church believes or teaches about Mary. It's important that you know what the Church actually teaches and equally important that you be able to articulate it. In this book, we hope to share with you *some* (though, not all) of what you "need to know" about the Blessed Virgin Mary: Mother of God, your Mother and the Queen of Heaven.

Put simply, Mary *is* Catholicism. She is the perfect disciple. She is everything we are called to be. While we'll never be perfect like Mary, our pursuit of Christ should lead us to saintliness like hers: rooted in humility, trust, service and love.

Life Teen is consecrated to the Blessed Virgin Mary. She is our guardian and our Mother. We ask her daily to pray with us and for us and we encourage you to ask Her to do the same for you.

A popular question from people, especially non-Catholics, is, "Why focus at all on Mary? Why not just focus on Jesus?"

Often, the question is asked with sincere intentions, but stems from an erroneous idea that Catholics take their attention off Jesus to focus on Mary.

At no time has the Catholic Church ever suggested taking the attention or focus off Christ. We as Catholics and Christians, are encouraged, implored and commanded to look to Christ and focus on Him in our prayers.

The misunderstanding comes when people think that Mary takes the place of Christ, which she does not. Nor does our invitation to Mary to pray for us, get in the way of Christ praying to God on our behalf.

Mary doesn't get in the way of Christ being our mediator to God. She enhances it.

When we pray, we invite Mary to join her prayers to ours, praying with us to Christ. Mary does not **and would not** do anything to divert the glory away from Jesus. She lived to glorify God. Anyone who disagrees should read **Luke 1:46-56**.

A few things I share with or ask people who pose this question to me:

When Mary came to Christ with a need (Jn. 2) did He respond to her? Yes.
Did Jesus hold Mary in high esteem, honoring her like a Son should? Yes.
Did Jesus give her to us as a mother (Jn. 19)? Yes.
Did Mary hold a place of honor in the early Church (Acts 1-2)? Yes.

Jesus is the ultimate prayer because He is the ultimate Pray-er. It tells us in Scripture (Gal. 2:20) that we become "little Christs" when we follow Him. We are called to imitate Christ in every way (1 Cor. 11:1). I want to be just like Jesus.

In prayer, ask Christ to grant you His Heart…

Pray:

I want to have the heart for God that you have, Jesus
I want to have the heart for the poor that you have, Jesus
I want to have the heart for sinners that you have, Jesus
I want to have the heart for the Word that you have, Jesus
I want to have the heart of mercy that you have, Jesus
I want to have the heart **for Your Mother** that you have, Jesus

I have yet to find someone who truly prays that prayer who does not hold Mary in the beautiful esteem that she, as the Mother of God, deserves.

May Our Lady bless you and may her prayers be with you as you read and pray through this book. She will hold you and walk with you, whenever you call upon her, always directing your path perfectly and gently back to her Son…like a good mother does.

Our Lady, pray for us!

- Bible Geek

What traits do you look for in a mother?
What traits would God look for...in a woman to mother His only Son?

The Scriptures may paint the portrait...but the brush belongs to God...and the Holy Spirit, is the most intimate Inspiration.

A woman created, a woman set apart.
A model of chastity, of inner beauty, of humility...of purity.
The golden vessel, chosen to carry the most important life the world will ever know...

Are we called everyday to live for God?
Did she model openness to God the Father, in every conceivable way?
Did she leave any doubt that God's will, was more important than hers...than mine?
Did she run when it was difficult? Or uncomfortable?

Did she trust in God even when the future was uncertain?
Did she hide Him away or share Him with the world?

Are we called to give the Lord our body AND soul?
Did she allow our Lord to live within her?
Did she know Jesus more intimately than anyone else on Earth, even His closest followers?
Did she hold Him, feed Him?
Did she guide and protect Him through his teenage years?
Did she stand by Him through it all?
Did she put God's will first, even until the last...the final moments?

Did His Mother ever abandon Him?
Now, as our Mother...would she ever abandon you... or abandon us?

God created her, He picked her, He descended upon her, He grew within Her...
He was held by Her, changed by Her, raised, and clothed by Her
Until one day, He was to be held by Her once again...

He listened to Her, loved Her...honored Her above any other, not because she wanted it, but because she deserves it...because *she is* different...because it was her "yes" to God, that set His brothers and sisters back on the right path...

It was her "fiat"...her yes, that *one phrase* that forever changed the world. "May it be done to me according to THY will" (Luke 1:38). One "Yes" opened the door to hope...hope in salvation, hope for life after death, hope for us

And, as a good older brother does, He shows us how to love Her, wants us to know Her, to respect Her...and trust Her as our own, so He entrusted us to Her, and then gave Her to each of us...so that we could know and experience the love that only a Mother can give, that only *His Mother*, created and chosen by God, *can give.*

He invites you to get to know Her, to meditate on Her heart, as a window into His own

He calls us to honor Her, modeling *Her* humility, Her openness, Her chastity, Her abandonment...

Just as our Blessed Mother reflects Jesus' light more radiantly and more fully than any other human in history...so we are called, as children of our Blessed Mother, as children of the *light*, to reflect and radiate the love and heart of Christ, to all the world...

In the *light*, it began with a courageous young teenage woman... In the *light*, God became man, and walked among us In the *light* of a bright Sunday sunrise, death was destroyed forever In the *light* of the Spirit's flame, a beautiful young Church was born

And it is in the *light* even today...this mysterious light of prayer, this light of hope, and through the light of our Lady's grace, that we truly become brother and sister, that we become sons and daughters, that we become the family of God that we were formed, designed and created to be...

One holy, pleasing and perfect family in and with the Spirit, gathered before the table, one with Blessed Father, His Blessed Son, and, indeed, our Blessed Mother...

"For what great nation is there that has gods so close to it as the LORD, our God, is to us whenever we call upon him? Take care and be earnestly on your guard not to forget the things which your own eyes have seen, nor let them slip from your memory as long as you live, but teach them to your children and to your children's children." - Deuteronomy 4:7,9

SITUATION EXPLAINED

In the United States we separate church and state, but the reality is that God is everywhere. We Christians know where to look.

SOLUTION OFFERED

Believe it or not, I learned about Jesus in public school; I just didn't realize it. Maybe church and state are not as separated as they seem. You remember the following nursery rhyme, courtesy of Mother Goose, right?

Mary had a little lamb, little lamb, little lamb
Mary had a little lamb, its fleece was white as snow.
Everywhere that Mary went, Mary went, Mary went
Everywhere that Mary went, the lamb was sure to go.

Well, the public school superintendents may not like this, but this little rhyme sounds pretty biblical to me. Let me show ya' what I mean:

"...Mary, of whom Jesus was born, who is called Christ." (Matthew 1:16).

"He looked at Jesus as he walked, and said, "Behold the Lamb of God!" (John 1:36).

"His appearance was like lightning and his clothing was white as snow." (Matthew 28:3). (Clothing in early Palestine was often referred to as "raiment" or "fleece")

"Now his parents went up to Jerusalem every year at the feast of Passover. And when he was twelve years old, they went up according to custom" (Luke 2:41-42)

"And the mother of Jesus was there; Jesus also was invited to the marriage" (John 2:1-2).

Mary did have a little lamb, we call him Jesus, and His life was as white and pure as snow. Jesus often was in the company of Mary, teaching us both respect for and obedience to our mother, as a good older brother does.

Robert Fulghum gave his book of essays the catchy title "All I Really Need to Know I Learned in Kindergarten (Ballantine, 2003). Maybe he's right. In kindergarten we learn to read, to write, to count. We learn to share, to listen and to respect others. We learn to play and to rest. We learn the most basic survival skills, really: patience, kindness and humility. These are all Christian virtues, the keys that unlock the doors to life in its later stages.

Thank God for simple nursery rhymes that remind us of all that is good and of just how simple the most profound truths of life can be. Virtues are rooted in Christ; they are "elementary" in that they are simple ideals that are taught publicly and privately.

I am thankful for all those who hold virtues and values dear, especially those who teach them to our young. They make a difference, and I'm sorry that I didn't realize it sooner. God bless them all.

SALVATION GIVEN
"For what great nation is there that has a god so near to it as the Lord our God is to us, whenever we call upon Him?...Only take heed, and keep your soul diligently, lest you forget the things which your eyes have seen, and lest they depart from your heart all the days of your life; make them known to your children and your children's children."
- Deuteronomy 4:7, 9

She is not just another
She is Mary, my Mother
She gave birth to my brother
She is like no other
Jesus, my Lord.

Bible Geek

*This reflection was originally published as a *Spread the Word* email through the Life Teen website. Visit www.lifeteen.com for an archive of hundreds of past reflections such as this one.

"Behold, you will conceive in your womb and bear a son, and you shall name him Jesus." - Luke 1:31

SITUATION EXPLAINED
Some days after waking up, life can take a funny turn can't it?

SOLUTION OFFERED
When Mary awoke that morning and began about her daily chores, do you think that she ever dreamed she would be visited by an angel that day? As she walked to the well maybe speaking with friends about her upcoming wedding to Joseph, do you think that she could fathom the turn her life would take? As she laid down on the mat in her home that night offering her evening prayers, do you think she had an inkling of how beautiful or of how difficult her life would turn out to be?

We have the benefit of looking at Mary in hindsight (from the future) and that view, at times, can get skewed. We know the Blessed Virgin Mary as the Mother of God, early Church disciple, faithful saint, wife and mother and the Queen of Heaven. We don't often associate Her with the humble teenage girl whose life was changed in an instant, and Who changed our lives forever through her "Yes" to life.

By "life" I don't just mean her willingness to participate in God's plan, or Her giving birth to the Messiah instead of choosing the easy way out, I mean Her YES to all that "life" carries with it, on a daily basis.

Everyone searches for "the meaning of life". Life, though, is not something to be found, but experienced, it is given by God not taken from Him. Life is our humanity at its finest. Life can be described as a search for truth, in which we deal with the pain, yearn for true love, remain hopeful for the outcome, (often) fear the unknown and (usually) don't like to sacrifice.

The truth can be uncomfortable at times; it causes us to be real with ourselves. The pain of broken relationships and lives can seem irreparable, so we lose hope. The love that we yearn for can appear unbearable, when it means discipline or surrender. The outcome that we pray for isn't always the solution that we most need. The fear that we retain is not from God, but from our inability to completely trust Him. At times, the sacrifice that seems "too great" was not God's for us, but ours for Him.

Sometimes the truth seems more than you and I can bear.
Sometimes the pain seems more than you and I can bear.
Sometimes the love seems more than you and I can bear.
Sometimes the outcome seems more than you and I can bear.
Sometimes the fear seems more than you and I can bear.
Sometimes the sacrifice seems more than you and I can bear.

But Mary bore all of these things...
She bore the truth, the pain, the love, the outcome, the fear and the sacrifice. She bore them when She bore Him, so that He might bear fruit in us, and so that we might bear fruit in this world.

She didn't bear Him to "bore" us. She bore Him to bring life, so that we might have life and have it "to the fullest" (John 10:10)...thus, insuring that our lives, yours and mine, would never become a bore.

Mary is the perfect example of how to live a life that is never boring. She didn't know what would happen next, She just said "Yes" to God at that moment, and then kept saying yes to Him with every turn. She jumped in the seat of the roller coaster car, threw Her hands in the air and said "take me where you want to take me"..."may it be done to Me according to Thy will." (Luke 1:38)

Like any parent, Mary would have chosen, in an instant, to take the pain upon herself, rather than watching her child go through it. If you have children, you understand. If you don't have children of your own...ask a parent, and see what they say.

Life takes on a different meaning in our humanity when we welcome in His divinity, like Mary did. Through the divine eyes of God, we view our lives from a timeless point of view, not from a temporary human perspective. Your life will be viewed much differently by people 2000 years from now, for instance, than you might presently view it. They might not see the hardships you went through or the struggles you had...kind of like when we look back at Biblical figures, like the way we look at our Mother Mary.

You will know the hardships, however, and so will God. You will also know the love and happiness, and so will God. And you will have a choice, maybe even today (though probably not with an angel) to answer and follow God's call for you...

The choice you will make...now that is life.

SALVATION GIVEN
"Behold, you will conceive in your womb and bear a son, and you shall name him Jesus." - Luke 1:31

The life given is only too much to "bear" when we try to bear it without the One who gifts it.

Bible Geek

*This reflection was originally published as a *Spread the Word* email through the Life Teen website. Visit www.lifeteen.com for an archive of hundreds of past reflections such as this one.

DOES GOD PLAY FAVORITES?

Q: Does God play favorites? Why would Mary, or the Saint's prayers hold more weight than our friends on earth? Why then do we pray the rosary?

There are a couple different ways to answer this question but the reason(s) behind the answers are based in the same truth.

First, God does not "play favorites" per se...that is a tricky phrase. When we are living in His grace, accepting His mercy and loving our God by trying to live a righteous life then we are in His favor, yes. Does that mean that someone who is not actively loving God is *loved less?* No. It means, like the Scriptures tell us, that we have *found favor with the Lord*...that favor fills Him with joy and us with peace. If that could be considered "playing favorites" then, so be it, I guess. Several important folks throughout Scripture, faithful people, "found favor" with the Lord, so you'd be in good company. To name a few:

Noah - *Genesis 6:8*
Moses - *Exodus 33:12-13, 16-17*
Esther - *Esther 8:5*
Mary - *Luke 1:30*

As for whether or not Mary and saints' prayers hold more weight than ours, the answer is yes - of course they do.

This is a very difficult truth for several folks to swallow. The difficulty lies more in ignorance than in pride, though. There are two things to consider here:

First, Mary, the saints and, indeed, all those souls in the Heavenly Host are in a state of perfect perfection, basking in the love, light and grace of God. They are in perfect union and communion with God, completely free from the stain of sin and not surrounded by sin *like you and I are* in this world.

Second, not only are we stuck in this world, but we are still battling pride, ego and any/every other self-involved area of our own humanity that has the ability to take our mind, eyes, and heart off our Lord Jesus Christ. That battle, no matter how valiantly fought, keeps us from experiencing the perfect love that we are designed to know **and will know** back home in Heaven.

Q: Is it wrong for me to pray the Our Father or the Hail Mary? My friend said that Catholics violate the Bible when they do, because we're not supposed to do repetitive prayers. Is that true?

No, it's not wrong to pray the Our Father or the Hail Mary, both prayers are scriptural and both honor and praise God. In fact, Jesus *commands* us to pray the Our Father:

"This is how you are to pray..." He tells us in **Matthew 6:9**.

Your friend is quoting a scripture verse that comes immediately before that passage above, which is from Matthew 6:7.

"In praying, do not babble like the pagans, who think that they will be heard because of their many words." (NAB)

or

"And in praying do not heap up empty phrases as the Gentiles do; for they think that they will be heard for their many words." (RSV)

or

"Don't recite the same prayer over and over as the heathen do, who think prayers are answered only by repeating them again and again"(LIB)

Notice how different these three translations are over the same verse? I put all three in to show how sometimes the *translation* of Bible that folks use can be part of the problem. Remember, the readings were first in Greek, and there's a lot of room for error, interpretation and personal agendas within some Biblical translations.

There is a misunderstanding on the part of your friend, however, when it comes to the verses above.

You see, the warning in the verses is against *meaningless* repetitions in prayer. Jesus is not saying that we should never have repetition in our prayers...in fact, by commanding us to pray the Our Father, He is encouraging us to pray the prayer frequently. It is not as though He was encouraging us to pray it just once.

Christ was warning us against thinking that "rattling off" prayers was what God the Father wanted. Christ was teaching us the difference between *quality and quantity*. Heartfelt and sincere repetition in prayer (like the rosary) can be a beautiful devotion that leads us into a more contemplative spirituality and a more disciplined prayer life amidst the distractions of this very loud and technological age.

We should pray the Our Father frequently, because it is the *ultimate PRAYER* given to us directly from the **ultimate PRAY-ER**, our Lord and Savior, Jesus Christ.

Several instances in Christ's life we witness Him observing forms of "repetitive prayer", like various forms of Jewish liturgical prayer (one example of this would be Passover, another would be the Feast of Tabernacles or Booths - read more in Mt. 26 or John 7-9).

I think about how often I might rush through grace before a meal, or sometimes rush through my prayers at night before bed...those are not repetitious in wording, but in habit, and could even be considered less "meaningful" than the rosary I prayed earlier in the day.

Think about it.

I hope this helped. If nothing else, your conversation with your friend should act as an important reminder about the need to always focus during prayer, and to meditate on Christ.

Like anything else in life, it is vital that we "say what we mean and mean what we say".

The Rosary is the most famous and most popular chaplet that we have as Catholics. A *chaplet* is a prayer devotion that commonly utilizes beads, it comes from a French word for "wreath" or "crown". While the structure and devotion of the rosary has its roots with the "desert fathers", it is **St. Dominic** who is historically credited with giving the structured gift of the Rosary to the greater Church.

In the Rosary we meditate on the life of Christ, gazing upon Him through the lens and window of Mary's soul. Since she is our Blessed Mother, gifted to us from His Cross (**Jn. 19:27**), it makes perfect sense that we would seek to look upon Christ in such an intimate and sinless way, as she does. The rosary draws us into more perfect discipleship, and focuses our prayer on the Trinity.

This a prayer on a group of beads developed as a way to teach the life of Christ and Mary to those who were not able to read. It was also developed to assist those who were not clergy in praying the Liturgy of the Hours, the prayer of the Church. In the prayer we take our intentions to Mary and show our honor and respect for her as the greatest of all the saints and an example to us all.

The Rosary is divided into four sets of Mysteries; **Joyful, Luminous, Sorrowful and Glorious**. It is intended as we pray each "Mystery" we meditate on the meaning of the event in the life of Christ and Mary and also on the event in our own lives.

Each Mystery has five decades and each decade is prayed upon in the following order: Our Father, Hail Mary and the Glory Be. There are other prayers that are added onto the beginning and end of the Rosary such as the Apostle's Creed and the Hail Holy Queen. The prayer order for the Rosary is below along with indications of specific beads:

JOYFUL
(MONDAY & SATURDAY)
The Annunciation
The Visitation
The Nativity of Jesus
The Presentation of Jesus
The Finding of Jesus

LUMINOUS
(THURSDAY)
The Baptism of Jesus
The Miracle at Cana
The Proclamation of the Kingdom
The Transfiguration
The Institution of the Eucharist

SORROWFUL
(TUESDAY & FRIDAY)
The Agony in the Garden
The Scourging at the Pillar
The Crowning of Thorns
The Carrying of the Cross
The Crucifixion

GLORIOUS
(WEDNESDAY & SUNDAY)
The Ressurection
The Ascension of Jesus
The Decent of the Holy Spirit
The Assumption of Mary
The Coronation of Mary

HOW TO PRAY THE ROSARY

Sign of the Cross

Apostles Creed

Our Father - 1st Bead
3 Hail Marys - 3 beads
Glory Be

1st Mystery:
Our Father - single bead
10 Hail Marys - 10 beads
Glory Be

2nd Mystery:
Our Father - single bead
10 Hail Marys - 10 beads
Glory Be

3rd Mystery:
Our Father - single bead
10 Hail Marys - 10 beads
Glory Be

4th Mystery:
Our Father - single bead
10 Hail Marys - 10 beads
Glory Be

5th Mystery:
Our Father - single bead
10 Hail Marys - 10 beads
Glory Be

Hail Holy Queen

It might be difficult for you to pray the rosary, because of the repetition of the prayers. I'll be honest with you, even though I pray it daily, it can still be tough for me sometimes. Repetition can have a soothing effect. The rhythm can be both a good thing and a bad thing (if you're like me). I have to work very hard to stay focused. Kneeling helps.   That being said, it is a great gift. All prayer is directed to the Father, through Jesus Christ.

The Rosary is directed to Christ, guided by His mother. We should be thankful for the guided, Scriptural prayers (the Our Father, Hail Mary, Glory Be), always. They help us pray. At times they are all I can verbalize, when I'm too tired, distracted or too much in pain to muster anything else, of my own.   And **remember** that we must always keep in mind Jesus' warning not to let our prayers become repetitious babbling or empty phrases (Mt. 6:7). Sometimes it helps to recite the prayers more slowly, to insure we are *praying and not just saying* the prayers.[1]

[1]Hart, Mark and Lemieux, Todd, *100 Things every Catholic Teen should know*, (Phoenix, AZ: Life Teen, Inc), 2007.

PRAYERS

APOSTLE'S CREED
I believe in God, the Father Almighty, Creator of heaven and earth and in Jesus Christ, His only Son, our Lord; Who was conceived by the Holy Spirit, born of the Virgin Mary, suffered under Pontius Pilate, was crucified, died, and was buried, He descended into hell; the third day He arose again from the dead; He ascended into Heaven, and sits at the right hand of God, the Father Almighty, from there He shall come to judge the living and the dead. I believe in the Holy Spirit, the Holy Catholic Church, the communion of saints, the forgiveness of sins, the resurrection of the body, and life everlasting. Amen.

THE LORD'S PRAYER
Our Father, Who art in Heaven, hallowed be Thy name; Thy Kingdom come, Thy will be done on earth as it is in Heaven. Give us this day our daily bread; and forgive us our trespasses as we forgive those who trespass against us; and lead us not into temptation, but deliver us from evil.   Amen.

HAIL MARY
Hail Mary, full of grace, the Lord is with thee, blessed art thou amongst women and blessed is the fruit of thy womb, Jesus. Holy Mary Mother of God, pray for us sinners now and at the hour of our death. Amen.

THE DOXOLOGY (GLORY BE)
All Glory be to the Father, the Son and the Holy Spirit, as it was in the beginning, is now and ever shall be, world without end. Amen.

SALVE REGINA (HAIL HOLY QUEEN)
Hail Holy Queen, Mother of Mercy, our life our sweetness and our hope. To thee do we cry, poor banished children of Eve; To thee do we send up our sighs, mourning and weeping in this valley of tears. Turn then, most gracious advocate, thine eyes of mercy toward us and after this our exile show unto us the blessed fruit of thy womb, Jesus. O clement, O loving, O sweet Virgin Mary! Pray for us oh Holy Mother of God, that we may be made worthy of the promises of Christ.

REFLECTIONS ON THE ROSARY

In the following pages we will take a look at all twenty mysteries of the Rosary. There are many great rosary resources that already exist that you should check out. You'd be wise to spend some time online and in your local Catholic bookstore or gift shop looking for books or reflections that help you enter into the rosary even more deeply. Some resources are more Scriptural, some more contemplative and others will help you focus your intentions.

What we have tried to do in the next twenty or thirty pages is to give you some questions and petitions to help guide and focus your prayers within each mystery. If your mind tends to "wander", hopefully these reflections will help keep you centered on the mystery at hand. If you don't struggle with focus than perhaps these reflections will help you to go deeper into the mysteries and how they relate to your everyday life.

These reflections are in no way complete, they are a starting point intended to bless your prayer experiences. May the Lord bless you and shower you with grace as you meditate on His life through the Blessed Mother's eyes.

JOYFUL
1. The Annunciation
2. The Visitation
3. The Nativity of Jesus
4. The Presentation of Jesus
5. The Finding of Jesus

LUMINOUS
1. The Baptism of Jesus
2. The Miracle at Cana
3. The Proclamation of the Kingdom
4. The Transfiguration
5. The Institution of the Eucharist

SORROWFUL
1. The Agony in the Garden
2. The Scourging at the Pillar
3. The Crowning with Thorns
4. The carrying of the Cross
5. The Crucifixion

GLORIOUS
1. The Resurrection
2. The Ascension of Jesus
3. The Descent of the Holy Spirit
4. The Assumption of Mary
5. The Coronation of Mary

JOYFUL MYSTERIES

THE ANNUNCIATION
Luke 1: 26-33, 38

THE VISITATION
Luke 1: 39-45

THE NATIVITY OF JESUS
Luke 2: 6-12

THE PRESENTATION OF JESUS
Luke 2: 25-32

THE FINDING OF JESUS
Luke 2: 41-50

ANNUNCIATION

OUR FATHER...

HAIL MARY...

God sees more in you than you see in yourself.

HAIL MARY...

How is God calling you to make Jesus present this day?

HAIL MARY...

God desires to bless and use you, even in your youth.

HAIL MARY...

Do you sometimes allow fear of the unknown affect your response to God's call?

HAIL MARY...

God has a plan for your life that might not be consistent with your plans.

ANNUNCIATION

HAIL MARY...

God's ways are not our ways.

HAIL MARY...

What virtue/characteristic do you see in Mary in this mystery that is most difficult for you to imitate?

HAIL MARY...

Do you believe that God will bring to fulfillment what He promises?

HAIL MARY...

Being faithful to God's plan is difficult at times.

HAIL MARY...

Would you say "yes" if you were Mary/Joseph?

GLORY BE...

VISITATION

OUR FATHER...

HAIL MARY...

Mary was greeted joyfully by Elizabeth. Do you share in others' joys?

HAIL MARY...

The Holy Spirit was upon John, even in the womb.

HAIL MARY...

In the presence of Jesus, John leaped in Elizabeth's womb. How are you moved in the presence of Jesus in the Eucharist?

HAIL MARY...

Mary gave thanks and glory to God, even though she did not fully under stand His plan.

HAIL MARY...

What does it mean (to you) to "magnify the Lord?"

VISITATION

HAIL MARY...

Are you magnifying Jesus by the way you live your daily life?

HAIL MARY...

John proclaimed the presence of Jesus without using words.

HAIL MARY...

How do your actions proclaim Jesus?

HAIL MARY...

Mary went and served Elizabeth.

HAIL MARY...

Is God calling you to service in some way?

GLORY BE...

THE NATIVITY

OUR FATHER...

HAIL MARY...

Mary said yes not only to one event, but a journey.

HAIL MARY...

What went through Joseph's mind when he held Jesus for the first time?

HAIL MARY...

What does God's humble birth teach us about Him?

HAIL MARY...

Did God supply a space when people wouldn't?

HAIL MARY...

Why were shepherds invited first and not nobler local men?

THE NATIVITY

HAIL MARY...

Would you have followed the star?

HAIL MARY...

Jesus depended on Mary for food, warmth and care.

HAIL MARY...

Mary is the Mother of God.

HAIL MARY...

Joseph and Mary trusted God. Do you?

HAIL MARY...

The King was laid upon a bed of straw, not a bed of silk. Do you ever let worldly comfort or materials affect your outlook on what is most important?

GLORY BE...

THE PRESENTATION

OUR FATHER...

HAIL MARY...

Mary and Joseph offered their only son back to God, for His glory.

HAIL MARY...

Do you give thanks to God for the things he gives you?

HAIL MARY...

How did Simeon know that Jesus was the Messiah?

HAIL MARY...

Have you been waiting for and looking for Jesus in your own life?

HAIL MARY...

God speaks to us constantly.

THE PRESENTATION

HAIL MARY...

How often do you stop and listen to God?

HAIL MARY...

How did it make Mary feel to hear prophecies that spoke of Her Son's suffering or death?

HAIL MARY...

If it was your child, what would you do if others spoke out against him?

HAIL MARY...

We own nothing, all good gifts come from God.

HAIL MARY...

Do you offer your gifts and blessings back to God or try to possess what is His?

GLORY BE...

FINDING JESUS IN THE TEMPLE

OUR FATHER...

HAIL MARY...

Why did Jesus feel the need to head back to the Temple?

HAIL MARY...

How often do you just listen to God?

HAIL MARY...

Would you have left your family to go spend time at church?

HAIL MARY...

Mary and Joseph only assumed that Jesus was with them. How many times in our lives do we assume things when God has other plans?

HAIL MARY...

Did Jesus speak first or listen first?

FINDING JESUS IN THE TEMPLE

HAIL MARY...

Do you ever feel like people don't expect much of you, because of your young age?

HAIL MARY...

How often do you stop worrying about the world and follow what God's plan is for you?

HAIL MARY...

If you are to be like Jesus, you must be obedient to your parents.

HAIL MARY...

How often do you trust your parents' guidance?

HAIL MARY...

God reveals His plan(s) for you...in His time, not yours.

GLORY BE...

LUMINOUS MYSTERIES

THE BAPTISM OF JESUS
Matthew 3: 13-17

THE MIRACLE AT CANA
John 2: 1-11

THE PROCLAMATION OF THE KINGDOM
Mark 1: 14-15

THE TRANSFIGURATION
Matthew 17: 1-8

THE INSTITUTION OF THE EUCHARIST
Matthew 26: 26-28

BAPTISM OF THE LORD

OUR FATHER...

HAIL MARY...

Do you believe that the Holy Spirit is with you?

HAIL MARY...

What gifts do you desire most from the Holy Spirit?

HAIL MARY...

You are God's beloved.

HAIL MARY...

The ministry of Jesus was not private; He came for you.

HAIL MARY...

What ministry has God designed you for?

BAPTISM OF THE LORD

HAIL MARY...

Do you view the Holy Spirit as a person or as a dove?

HAIL MARY...

John the Baptist's life pointed to Jesus. Does yours do the same?

HAIL MARY...

How is God calling you to point your family to the Lord?

HAIL MARY...

Baptism reveals God's desire for you to be part of His family.

HAIL MARY...

Say a prayer for your godparents.

GLORY BE...

THE WEDDING AT CANA

OUR FATHER...

HAIL MARY...

The disciples joined Mary and Jesus at the wedding feast.

HAIL MARY...

You are invited to Jesus' wedding feast, the Mass.

HAIL MARY...

Mary reminds us, "Do whatever He tells you".

HAIL MARY...

Do you listen to what God is calling you to do?

HAIL MARY...

Jesus turns the water into wine. Do you believe that God will work miracles in your own life?

THE WEDDING AT CANA

HAIL MARY...

What miracles do you need in your life?

HAIL MARY...

Do your desires seek out God's will or your own?

HAIL MARY...

Jesus produces an abundance of wine. He wants to shower His gifts upon you in abundance.

HAIL MARY...

Jesus honors the request of His Mother. Do you invite Mary to pray with you?

HAIL MARY...

Mary brought the situation to Jesus' attention and trusted in how He would act.

GLORY BE...

THE PROCLAMATION OF THE KINGDOM

OUR FATHER...

HAIL MARY...

When Christ came, the Kingdom came with Him.

HAIL MARY...

"The Kingdom of God is at hand. Repent and believe in the Gospel".
Mark 1:15

HAIL MARY...

Repent means to turn away from sin and to turn to God.

HAIL MARY...

What do you need to repent of?

HAIL MARY...

How are you going to avoid those sins in the future?

THE PROCLAMATION OF THE KINGDOM

HAIL MARY...

How can you turn even more to God?

HAIL MARY...

Do you believe in the Gospel, really believe in it?

HAIL MARY...

Jesus' kingdom is not of this world. Do you desire things of this world or His kingdom?

HAIL MARY...

What worldly desires or goals do you need to let go of to grab hold of God?

HAIL MARY...

Do you trust in God's will for your life, completely?

GLORY BE...

THE TRANSFIGURATION

OUR FATHER...

HAIL MARY...

Jesus took his disciples to pray. Prayer is essential to following Christ.

HAIL MARY...

When do you "get away" from the daily grind and go to pray with Jesus?

HAIL MARY...

During prayer they had a powerful experience of God.

HAIL MARY...

Moses and Elijah risked their lives to follow God and share His message.

HAIL MARY...

Picture this scene in your head. What does it look like in your imagination?

THE TRANSFIGURATION

HAIL MARY...

Where do you see God's glory in the Church?

HAIL MARY...

Do you see God's glory in your everyday life?

HAIL MARY...

"This is my chosen Son, listen to Him." Luke 9:35

HAIL MARY...

What needs to change so you can listen more closely to God?

HAIL MARY...

When you focus on the face of Jesus, do you look away or stare more deeply?

GLORY BE...

INSTITUTION OF THE EUCHARIST

OUR FATHER...

HAIL MARY...

The command was, "Take and eat" not "take and understand." - C.S. Lewis

HAIL MARY...

At the Last Supper, Jesus celebrated the first Mass.

HAIL MARY...

Do you fully participate in Mass every Sunday?

HAIL MARY...

Do you remember the readings from last Sunday?

HAIL MARY...

Do you sit as close, listen as closely, sing as gratefully as you ought?

INSTITUTION OF THE EUCHARIST

HAIL MARY...

Jesus sacrificed Himself for us, how do you sacrifice yourself for Him?

HAIL MARY...

Eucharist literally means "thanksgiving".

HAIL MARY...

Jesus gave thanks, what do you have to be thankful for in your life?

HAIL MARY...

Do you spend adoration time alone with Jesus before the Blessed Sacrament?

HAIL MARY...

Say a prayer for your parish priests, in thanksgiving for their vocation to the priesthood.

GLORY BE...

SORROWFUL MYSTERIES

THE AGONY IN THE GARDEN
Luke 22: 39-46

THE SCOURGING AT THE PILLAR
Mark 15: 6-15

THE CROWNING WITH THORNS
John 19: 1-8

THE CARRYING OF THE CROSS
John 19: 16-22

THE CRUCIFIXION
John 19: 25-30

AGONY IN THE GARDEN

OUR FATHER...

HAIL MARY...

God is calling you to sit and pray with Him. What distractions fill your mind as you prepare to pray this Rosary.

HAIL MARY...

"My soul is sorrowful..." (Mark 14:34) Tell Christ how your soul is sorrowful or distressed.

HAIL MARY...

Share with your Father, like Christ, the cup (situation) you wish could be removed from your life at this time?

HAIL MARY...

"Not what I will but what Your will." (Mark 14:36) God desires that you trust in His will, and not your own.

HAIL MARY...

God prays that you will live in His light and not live in the darkness.

AGONY IN THE GARDEN

HAIL MARY...

Pray that you can forgive someone who abandoned you in your hour of need.

HAIL MARY...

We all know the pain that is felt when someone betrays us. Find it in your heart to forgive someone who betrayed you.

HAIL MARY...

Pray for souls lost in darkness or depression, who do not know God's love or mercy.

HAIL MARY...

"Watch and pray that you may not undergo the test. The Spirit is willing but the flesh is weak." (Mark 14:38) Pray for grace in times of temptation.

HAIL MARY...

May the example of our Mother Mary instill in us the gift of perseverance and patience in seeking the will of God.

GLORY BE...

THE SCOURGING AT THE PILLAR

OUR FATHER...

HAIL MARY...

Lord, forgive me for all the times I have torn people down with my words or actions.

HAIL MARY...

"For he (Pontius Pilate) knew it was out of envy that the chief priests handed him over." (Mark 15:10) Lord, reveal to me the people of whom I am envious?

HAIL MARY...

Pray for God's forgiveness for both the things we do and fail to do.

HAIL MARY...

When have you failed to speak for the truth or defend Christ?

HAIL MARY...

The Lord calls you to be a voice for those with no voice.

THE SCOURGING AT THE PILLAR

HAIL MARY...

When have you persecuted Christ in another?

HAIL MARY...

God calls you to stand strong in times of difficulties and persecution.

HAIL MARY...

Jesus suffered for the sins of all, including your sins.

HAIL MARY...

God allowed Himself to suffer.

HAIL MARY...

Suffering reveals true love.

GLORY BE...

THE CROWNING OF THORNS

OUR FATHER...

HAIL MARY...

Lord, reveal to me all the ways I live for the world and not for You.

HAIL MARY...

When have you pierced another with mockery, sarcasm or hurtful words?

HAIL MARY...

Pray for forgiveness and healing for the times you have used hurtful words or committed hurtful actions.

HAIL MARY...

Christ the King's crown wasn't made of earthly gold, but thorns.

HAIL MARY...

Living for the Kingdom of Heaven will get you persecuted on earth.

THE CROWNING OF THORNS

HAIL MARY...

God alone is to be glorified and praised!

HAIL MARY...

Who in your life lives boldly for Christ, regardless of mockery? Pray for them.

HAIL MARY...

Mother Mary, humble and purify me of all things that I have placed before my God.

HAIL MARY...

Lord, open my eyes to the people I mock and insult daily.

HAIL MARY...

Lord, allow me to find it in my heart to love those who mock and insult me.

GLORY BE...

THE CARRYING OF THE CROSS

OUR FATHER...

HAIL MARY...

The Lord is calling you to follow His example, to be strong in the darkness.

HAIL MARY...

Do you trust that He has not abandoned you?

HAIL MARY...

Give me the courage, Lord, to accept the cross I am called to carry.

HAIL MARY...

God loves Jesus perfectly, and still allowed Jesus to suffer.

HAIL MARY...

God loves you perfectly. If you suffer it doesn't mean God has forgotten about you.

THE CARRYING OF THE CROSS

HAIL MARY...

The Lord send you people, like Simon, to help carry your crosses.

HAIL MARY...

Who are you helping to carry their cross?

HAIL MARY...

Like the weeping woman, give me the courage to follow you when the crowd is jeering and cursing Your holy name.

HAIL MARY...

Lord, when I fall, give me the strength to keep walking and to keep seeking you.

HAIL MARY...

What are the burdens or "crosses" that come from your own sin, that Christ wants to remove?

GLORY BE...

THE CRUCIFIXION

OUR FATHER...

HAIL MARY...

"Father, forgive them for they know not what they do." (Luke 23:34) Lord, allow me to forgive others when they seek to hurt me.

HAIL MARY...

Jesus chose the cross. Nails didn't hold Jesus down, they held Him up.

HAIL MARY...

The salvation Jesus offers from the cross will take away all pain and suffering.

HAIL MARY...

"Jesus, remember me when you come into Your kingdom." (Mark 23:42)

HAIL MARY...

Jesus, be my Savior, today and forever!

THE CRUCIFIXION

HAIL MARY...

"I thirst" (John 19:28) May I thirst for You alone, Lord Jesus.

HAIL MARY...

Like Mary and the disciples who followed to Calvary, may we continually keep our eye on Christ in the midst of an evil generation.

HAIL MARY...

Have you placed Christ on the cross this day?

HAIL MARY...

Are you the thief asking merely for intervention or for total salvation?

HAIL MARY...

"Today, you will be with me in paradise" (Mark 23:43). Jesus wants you in Heaven.

GLORY BE...

GLORIOUS MYSTERIES

THE RESURRECTION
Mark 16: 1-7

THE ASCENSION OF JESUS
Luke 24: 45-53

THE DESCENT OF THE HOLY SPIRIT
Acts 2: 1-7, 11

THE ASSUMPTION OF MARY
Luke 1: 46-55

THE CORONATION OF MARY
Revelations 12: 1-17, Judith 13: 18-20

THE RESSURECTION

OUR FATHER...

HAIL MARY...

If Jesus didn't rise from the dead, you are not saved from death.

HAIL MARY...

In what areas of your life do you feel dead or "entombed"?

HAIL MARY...

Invite God to resurrect those "dead areas" of your life.

HAIL MARY...

How did Mary feel on Good Friday?

HAIL MARY...

Do you struggle to trust God when you are suffering?

THE RESSURECTION

HAIL MARY...

What was Mary thinking on Easter morning?

HAIL MARY...

Are you ever surprised by God's goodness?

HAIL MARY...

Do the people in your world believe that Jesus is God?

HAIL MARY...

Do your moral choices demonstrate someone who believes Jesus is alive?

HAIL MARY...

Do you run out into the day passionately excited to tell people the "good news"?

GLORY BE...

THE ASCENSION

OUR FATHER...

HAIL MARY...

Do you believe that Jesus is only "in Heaven" or, also, on earth?

HAIL MARY...

What did it look like when He ascended?

HAIL MARY...

Heaven is not just for God, the angels and saints. Heaven is for you.

HAIL MARY...

Do you see Heaven as your true home?

HAIL MARY...

What needs to change in your life now to insure Heaven or eternity?

THE ASCENSION

HAIL MARY...

Your holy example will inspire others to live a holier life.

HAIL MARY...

The apostles were nervous about "what to do next".

HAIL MARY...

Didn't Jesus make His desires and our instructions clear enough before the Ascension? What does He want from you?

HAIL MARY...

The angels told the disciples to quit standing there and get to work.

HAIL MARY...

You have work to do for Jesus.

GLORY BE...

DESCENT OF THE HOLY SPIRIT AT PENTECOST

OUR FATHER...

HAIL MARY...

God meets you where you are.

HAIL MARY...

Are you open to where the Holy Spirit calls you to go?

HAIL MARY...

The Holy Spirit destroys fear with boldness.

HAIL MARY...

Are you open to speaking what the Spirit prompts you to say?

HAIL MARY...

The Holy Spirit is power.

DESCENT OF THE HOLY SPIRIT AT PENTECOST

HAIL MARY...

The Holy Spirit is within you.

HAIL MARY...

Invite the Holy Spirit to breathe in you and through you.

HAIL MARY...

Do you see clearly where the Holy Spirit is leading you?

HAIL MARY...

Give me the courage to follow your way, Holy Spirit.

HAIL MARY...

The Spirit is always before you and burning within you.

GLORY BE...

ASSUMPTION OF MARY

OUR FATHER...

HAIL MARY...

Mary always is, was and will be - full of grace.

HAIL MARY...

Mary didn't ascend into heaven, she was assumed.

HAIL MARY...

Mary is unlike any other human who ever walked the face of the planet.

HAIL MARY...

The love of Mary is truly glorious.

HAIL MARY...

Mary's body never experienced corruption.

ASSUMPTION OF MARY

HAIL MARY...

Mary is the perfect vessel of God.

HAIL MARY...

How often to you reflect upon Mary's importance?

HAIL MARY...

The grace of God overflowed from Mary onto all of Her children.

HAIL MARY...

Mary is a constant example and presence of faithfulness.

HAIL MARY...

God honors Mary's sacrifice and surrender.

GLORY BE...

CORONATION OF MARY, QUEEN OF HEAVEN

OUR FATHER...

HAIL MARY...

The Kingdom of Heaven praised Mary in her perfection.

HAIL MARY...

Mary's crown wasn't requested, only deserved.

HAIL MARY...

Even as a Queen, humility still fills Mary's being.

HAIL MARY...

Picture Mary, your Mother, enthroned in Heaven.

HAIL MARY...

Doesn't God honor Mary's requests?

CORONATION OF MARY, QUEEN OF HEAVEN

HAIL MARY...

Mary was set apart on earth as she is in Heaven.

HAIL MARY...

Christ welcomed Mary as Mother and Queen.

HAIL MARY...

The Holy family on earth is the Royal family of Heaven.

HAIL MARY...

Honor Mary the way Christ honored her.

HAIL MARY...

A lifetime of humble sacrifice is met with eternal glory and celebration.

GLORY BE...

It's great to be Catholic. We have the Sacraments and Christ's true presence in the Eucharist. We have the Bible, the Sacred Scriptures which the Catholic Church, Herself, put together for you. We have the Mass, where we enter into God's throne room and participate in the re-presentation of Christ's sacrifice in the upper room and upon Calvary. We have the Pope...who's just cool. We have a special relationship with the Blessed Virgin Mary, who Jesus gave us as our own Mother (Jn. 19:26-27). The list goes on and on...

One of the greatest gifts you are given as a Roman Catholic is that you are part of a huge family in the Communion of Saints.

So, how about we take a minute to answer some of the most common questions and misconceptions regarding praying with Mary and saints? After that, we'll give you some specific saints that you might want to learn a little more about during your teenage and young adult years.

1. Is it wrong to pray to Mary and the Saints?

Just to make it very clear up front, Catholics and Protestants believe and command that we are to pray to God constantly, and without reservation. We agree on that, absolutely.

The Catholic Church does not and has not encouraged folks to take their attention or prayer off or away from Jesus. The confusion on the part of most non-Catholics stems from a misinterpretation of what is truly happening when a Catholic invites Mary (and/or the saints in Heaven) to pray to Christ on their behalf. Let's dive right in...

2. It's important to explain that there are different natures of prayer.

A prayer is a petition...

Prayer to God includes worship (that He is obviously due).

Prayer with Mary and the saints includes honor, not worship. A prayer is a petition, like in old English when someone would say something like, "I pray thee, tell me to what thine problem is?" or "What, pray tell, is the problem?"

3. The saints in Heaven are alive and are perpetually in prayer.

They are absolutely living in Heaven, just as you and I live, but to an even fuller extent, in that they are back home with God. They are far closer to God than we are, as sinful humans walking the earth. The saints in Heaven are free of all sin which hinders our prayers (Mt. 17:20, 1 Jn. 3:22, Ps. 66:18) and they are in a totally perfect union with God. It's less a matter of praying to Mary as much as it is praying with or through Mary.

4. We are commanded and encouraged in scripture to pray for others and for one another.

Where most people get confused, however, is that they quote something like 1 Timothy 2:5 speaking about how Christ is the only Mediator between man and God (which the Catholic Church agrees with, by the way) but they never take the time to read or really take to heart the four verses immediately preceding that verse, 1 Timothy 2:1-4.

5. It is important to realize what we are and are not saying when we say that we ask our Mother Mary and the saints to pray for us.

Christ is the primary mediator, and prayers on our behalf to Christ by either saints living in Heaven, or friends living on Earth (fulfilling the command in scripture to pray for each other) would be called a secondary mediation. That's what St. Paul is talking about throughout his epistles, like in Romans 15:30-32, Col. 1:4,9-10 and 2 Cor. 1:10...(want a couple more? Try Romans 10:1, and 2 Tim. 1:3).

When St. Paul (in his first letter to Timothy) asks us to pray for one another, he is asking us to assume a role of secondary mediation. When I pray to Christ on your behalf, as your friend, I am doing the same thing the saints do for me when I ask them to pray to Jesus on my own behalf...to join their prayers to mine, en route to Christ.

Since they're closer to Him than I am, it makes even more sense for them to pray for me, than my earthly friends. Hebrews chapter 12 speaks about "the cloud of witnesses" referring to what we call the Communion of Saints; take the time to read the chapter, paying particular attention to 12:1, 12:18-19 and 12:22-24. Further, go to Revelation 5:8, 14...then go on to Rev 6:10 and 8:3-4.

Q: I have a ton of questions about saints. My friends who aren't Catholic are saying it's bad and even sinful to pray to saints. They're saying that there's nothing special about saints that their stories aren't true and that the Church makes up stuff and that saints are no more important than anyone else. Why do we pray to them? Why do some have such random things they're patrons of? Why do some bodies not decompose? What is a halo, exactly? What are relics? Why does the Church let our attention be put on saints and off of Jesus?

A: Okay, that's a whole lot of questions you crammed in there. Let's take a stab...

Just to set the record straight...saints are not more important than Jesus. The Church has never said that, taught that or thought that. If someone claims that, tell them to show you where...'cause it just isn't true.

There's too much about the saints to answer in just a couple pages. Hopefully here in *Saintbook*, you'll find a wealth of knowledge and guidance in which you can explore and learn more on your own. Be sure to pay special attention to Scripture and Catechism (CCC) references. Also, take some time to check out some of the websites and books referenced on our Life Teen website at www.lifeteen.com. There are countless resources that will serve as an invaluable tool for you.

Here goes:

1. What is a saint?

The word *saint* comes from the Latin word **Sanctus** which means "holy" or "set apart". St. Paul first said it (Phil. 4:21) to mean all of the *faithful* early Christians. Our Church teaches that the saints occupy a hallowed (holy, special) place in Heaven. That place is in the presence of the Beatific vision... basically, front row center in God's throne room.

The Church doesn't say that every saint is named...far from it – the ones we officially call "saints" are joined by countless others who lived "saintly" lives but whom we haven't investigated and titled "saints", officially. By best estimates, there are over 10,000 saints that are currently named…again, most saints are not named on earth but are known in Heaven.

In fact, there are living, breathing saints around you right now…and not just in the Blessed Teresa of Calcutta types that you see on television. There are saints in your own parish and/or neighborhood, very likely. Most of them will never enjoy "the title" on earth, but that's okay - truly saintly people would never want the title, anyway.

2. How does someone get the title of saint?

The title of saint is conferred on someone after what is called the canonization process. The process was most formalized by Pope Alexander III in the 12th century. He restricted the perigatuve of canonization to the Holy See (Vatican authority). Canonization means 'being raised to the full honors of the altar'. (You can read more about this in the Catechism of the Catholic Church #828).

Basically, if you had someone you wanted to suggest for sainthood, you and a group would send a report to the Congregation for the Causes of Saints (a Vatican group).

That congregation would research the candidate's virtues, life, etc to see if the person should be recommended or not. If the Pope accepts the report from the congregation, the person in question is titled, Venerable. (Venerable means "accorded great respect due to heroic character".)

Once venerable there are several more steps in the process in which the person's life is exhaustively researched and examined. If alive, witnesses are contacted who knew the deceased, various people can come forward to raise objections, debates can ensue and discussions had. Also, at least two miracles must occur and be directly attributed to that saint's intercession to God. Once that happens (if and when it does), the person is "beatified" in a ceremony by the Pope at St. Peter's in Rome, and the person is declared "blessed."

After a period of time and a few more miracles…the "blessed" will be recommended for canonization and, eventually, named a saint at a ceremony in Rome (although there have been some canonization ceremonies that took place outside of the Vatican – i.e. in Korea in 1984).

3. Why do Catholics pray with/to saints, doesn't that go against the Bible?

NO. Asking for intercessory prayer does not go against Scripture. In fact, the Bible encourages intercessory prayer. Normally, when people take issue with the Blessed Virgin Mary's role or the Communion of Saints, it is rooted in a misunderstanding of intercession, how it works, the primacy of Jesus (which is never in question) and what we're asking of the saints on our behalf.

Jesus Christ is our mediator and intercessor...that is what our Church teaches. That being clearly stated and understood, our Mother and brothers/sisters in Heaven are powerful intercessors of prayer for us – secondary intercessors... that join their prayers to ours, putting them at the feet of Jesus, for His glory.

Throughout this *Saintbook*, you'll find more information regarding this topic. Keep on reading.

4. What is a halo, exactly?

It's a popular video game...next question.
Okay – that was stupid.

A halo is a "circle of light" that is seen in artistic interpretations of saints (or saintly people). It was originally used in Greek and Roman depictions of other gods, but the early Christians began using it in connection with the light of Christ...that's why, over the centuries, the halo began being seen and used in artistic representations of the Saints – to show how they radiate with the light of Christ, and reflect His light to the world.

5. Why do we have patron saints, and why do we have patrons for such "random" things?

While the patronages of certain saints do appear a little "random" on the surface, it's actually quite cool. Let me explain (briefly).

Saints had hobbies and interests, just like you and me. St. Ignatius Loyola played pool. St. Charles Borromeo loved to play chess. St. Jerome played the fiddle. St. Lydwina was an ice skater. You get the idea.

Now, how does someone become a "patron" saint? Well, take St. Lydwina, for instance. She was 16 years old when she had a freak accident while ice skating. What began as a broken rib led to gangrene (it was the 14th century) and eventually, she was paralyzed. But she offered her paralysis and suffering to God, and continued to pray and meditate.

Her devotion to the Holy Eucharist grew, even though she was confined to her bed, and over time, she was given visions of Heaven and Purgatory and she was visited by various saints. Tradition even holds that many miracles were performed at her bedside, and many healings. So, she is the patron saint for invalids, the homebound, and ice skaters.

Now, we have a patron saint for just about everything under the sun (Eccl. 1:9), and it's a great thing. It's almost guaranteed that anything you like to do, there is a patron saint for – someone who lived a holy life (worthy of sainthood), and did so enjoying the same thing you do.

In addition, patrons are given to us for special situations (death, illness, divorce, etc), special places (your hometown or native country), or special needs (hopeless causes, schoolwork, lost articles, etc.).

Spend sometime online to learn more about different patrons. I'll bet you'll find some saints with whom you have a lot in common.

6. What are relics and what do they have to do with saints?

Relics are special things associated with saints. While there are literally millions of relics in the world, not all are "official relics". In fact, our Church is really careful about officially naming something a relic, and rarely guarantees that a relic is authentic.

There are different stages or "classes" or relics.

First class relics are actual body parts of Saints, like bones or limbs...or tongues. (Gross sounding – I know, but really interesting)

Second class relics are usually something used by the saint, like books or rosaries or some other special object...clothing would also usually count as a second class relic.

Third class relics are usually anything touched by the saint or touched to a first class relic.

Many altars (in churches just like yours) actually have a small piece of bone from a saint placed/built within them. Ask your parish priest if yours does…

7. Why do we choose a saint name for Confirmation?

The receiving of a name at Confirmation has a number of different sources in the history of the Church. But the biggest one comes from the idea of a name being associated with a change of life. When Jesus told Simon that his new name was now Peter (Matthew 16:18), it was because his role was changing and he was going to be asked to take on a role of leadership. When Saul had his great conversion, the risen Lord gave him the name Paul (Acts 13:9). And there are a number of others that we see this happen to as well because there is a power in a name. If we look back at the Old Testament, to name some-one was to have ownership of them, which is why when Moses asked God in the burning bush who was sending him to Pharaoh, God didn't give him his name, He gave him his title, "I am who am" (Exodus 3:14). So to take on a new name at confirmation also carries with it the idea that you are asking for the Lord to change you. To take ownership of you like He's never done before and to live your faith more fully and with more life than you ever could've imagined.

The name of the saint also should have some significance to you, that particular saint is an example of the type of holiness you would like. Some people take St. Francis because they want to be kind to animals, or some people take St. Joseph because they want to be as holy as he was, or some people take St. Monica because she had such patience with her children, and the list could go on. The idea is to pick somebody who says something about you. And when you stand before the Bishop the day of your Confirmation and you tell him your name, say it with a pride and with a conviction and with the knowledge that the Holy Spirit is going to change you forever.

8. What about the "weird" things like saints' bodies not decomposing, what's up with that?

Some saints have "supernatural", inexplicable miracles associated with their bodies and senses, they include bilocation, incorruptibility, levitation, locution, the odor of sanctity and the stigmata, to name a few.

It's interesting that not much is reported about these miracles, but they are real. Literally, thousands of witnesses attest to seeing things like levitation, seeing saints in two places at once (bilocation), touching the stigmata and watching blood flow from the wounds in the hands and feet (the wounds of Christ), and many, myself included, have seen incorruptible saints.

If you ever have the chance to travel, especially throughout Europe, you might have the opportunity to see an incorruptible saint – their body doesn't decay at the normal rate. That incorruptibility is seen as a sign of their incredible spirituality – St. Bernadette, St. Clare of Assisi, St. Vincent de Paul, Pope Pius X, St. John Vianney, St. Frances Cabrini – the list goes on and on. Most of these saints have been dead for several hundred years, but their bodies are in amazing condition.

And it's not just for "official saints" or saints from centuries ago. I saw Blessed John XXIII's body on my last trip to the Vatican. It was exumed and exposed in a clear coffin in the middle of St. Peter's Basilica...incorrupt and looking great after over 40 years in the tomb. That was cool.

9. Where can I read more about the saints?

There are tons of great websites online, but be careful, some of them are more accurate than others. Check out the "References and Resources" page at the end of this book.

Fr. Butler's Lives of the Saints is generally considered the finest single compilation on the saints ever put together. There's probably a volume at your parish...maybe even in your home, if your parents went to parochial school.

10. Why should saints matter to me today, in the 21st century?

Many times, Catholics (young and old) will question why the saints are important or how they are relevant in modern times. While technology and times change, life is a constant, as are temptation, sin, grace and holiness.

As the song says, "the saints are just the sinners who fell down...and got up."

We can always learn from the saints. It is essential that we never lose our sense of discipleship (literally, "student-ship"). We must keep learning from our past, and our families. The saints are our older brothers and sisters in the faith.

BONUS

Is it true that some saints have their "saint title" taken away?

Oh yeah, we're bumping them right out of Heaven! We're telling them to pack their bags and go. They've had the cozy life too long, they need to go get real jobs. No, they are not "de-sainting" anyone in actuality. The teaching on someone receiving the title of saint means that they have made it into the glories of Heaven, we can't kick anyone out. Now, if you're referring to saints on a calendar of saints, holy days throughout the course of the year, that is a different story. Because the calendar of saints can be changed over time and is different in different countries, there are different saints that are more nationally known here in the United States than in other parts of the world. There are also different calendars of saints of Religious Orders that are special to them, like the Franciscans and the Jesuits and so forth.

So, people can be taken off of the calendar of saints, but no one stops being a saint once they've made it. In the case of someone like St. Christopher, he's never stopped being a saint; he's just not on the calendar of saints anymore. So don't worry about your favorite saints, they're not going to be kicked out of heaven or anything. I hope that this helps. Please know that you're always in my prayers.

It's not weird to respect saints, to talk about them, study them, honor them or invite them to pray with and for you.

What is weird is claiming to be a Christian and not desire holiness and intimacy with Christ to such an intense level, that you would stop at nothing to live the life of a saint, yourself.

Live the life of a saint this and every day and someday you'll be one. You might even have a statue in your honor...not because you want it, but because your life deserves it.

What's the purpose of stained glass windows?

"While you have the light, believe in the light, so that you may become sons of the light." - Jn. 12:36

SITUATION EXPLAINED
What is the purpose of stained glass in Church? Ever think about it?
In case you've never heard the following story, I wanted to share it with you.

SOLUTION OFFERED
It was Sunday morning, and as always, a young family made their way into Mass. A beautiful little six-year-old girl, the youngest, sat amazed, gazing up at the ceilings, the candles, the statues, and the crucifix. Then she noticed an incredible array of colored light beaming onto the floor in front of her. Her eyes immediately scaled the walls to find the source. She saw the brilliant, early morning sun shining through the stained glass window.

She asked her father, "Daddy, who are those people in the colored windows?"

"Those are the saints, sweetheart, people who lived for God and who loved Him very much."

The young girl nodded in approval. She kept her eyes glued to the stained glass for the remainder of the Mass.

A couple years later the same girl sat in her Catholic elementary school religion class. "Who are the saints?" the teacher asked the students at the beginning of the lesson. No one in the class raised a hand, with the exception of the little girl. The teacher called on her, and she humbly rose to answer the question. "So who are the saints?" The teacher asked again.

"The saints are the ones the light shines through," the little girl innocently replied.

Remember, the saints were ordinary people who got tired, who got hungry, who even got annoyed. They got sick, they got headaches, they made mistakes, they sinned, and they went through temptations, too...just like you and me. They dealt with the same types of situations, people and annoyances that you and I struggle with every day. The big difference is *how* they responded to God's call and *how* they chose to live in the midst of hardship.

You can be a saint. I could be a saint. We are all *called* to be saints. Don't ever think, "That could never be me." It can be; "With God nothing will be impossible" (Lk. 1:37).

Start today. Smile. Serve. Affirm. Let the joy of Christ radiate within you. Really try, in a new way, to allow the light of Christ, the awesomeness of God, to shine through you...to the wonder and amazement of all who see it. *That* would be a beautiful gift...one that shouldn't be reserved just for church.

SALVATION GIVEN
"While you have the light, believe in the light, so that you may become sons of the light." - Jn. 12:36

Make your life a "stained glass" work of art to a world in need.

Bible Geek

*This reflection was originally published as a *Spread the Word* email through the Life Teen website. Visit www.lifeteen.com for an archive of hundreds of past reflections such as this one.

Q: Do Catholics worship statues?

This is one of the most common misconceptions about the Catholic faith. Many well-intentioned, God-loving Christians of various denominations have heard this mistruth from trusted but ignorant teachers over the years, or have read it in books that claim to "expose" what they believe to be the Catholic faith. Unfortunately, as with most misconceptions, these conclusions are drawn with little or no true understanding of the faith or of the practice, or the purpose in question.

Before I answer this question, I'd like to quote a wonderful man of God, the late Archbishop Fulton Sheen, who said, "There are not one hundred people in this world who hate Catholicism, but there are millions who hate what they mistakenly believe Catholicism to be." So, is worshipping a statue wrong? Yes. The Roman Catholic Church teaches that it is wrong, in line with the Sacred Scriptures as it states in Exodus 20:4-5, "You shall not carve idols for yourselves in the shape of anything in the sky above or on the earth below or in the waters beneath the earth; you shall not bow down before them or worship them".

That being said...there are several places in the Bible where God commissions statues and images for religious usage:

• Exodus 25:10-22
• 1 Kings 6:23; 7:13-51
• Numbers 21:6-9
• Judges 17:1-6

Is God sending Two Different Messages? Not necessarily...keep reading. God ordered His children to construct these statues and images, but He did not intend for His children to worship them. God was using the images to help them to recall situations, to see places as holy and set apart, to help them to open their minds and hearts and turn them back to God. You see, an **image is not an idol**. There is a difference. "An image is simply a spiritual 'visual aid' that is used by the faithful to increase their spirit of prayerfulness and devotion to God. An idol, on the other hand, is an image that is worshipped by the unfaithful in place of the one true God (i.e., the 'golden calf' described in Ex. 32:7-8)." In the Old Testament, images of God were forbidden because folks had not yet seen God in human form. In the New Testament, God HAS taken on human form...an image that we can see.

"He (Jesus) is the image of the invisible God..." - **Colossians 1:15**

"For in Jesus dwells the whole fullness of the Deity, bodily..." - **Colossians 2:9**

"What was from the beginning, what we have heard, what we have seen with our eyes, what we looked upon and touched with our hands concerns the Word of life - for the life was made visible..." - **1 John 1:1-2**

When we profess that Jesus Christ is Lord, we must remember that we are professing the Incarnation...that is, that God became flesh...flesh in human form, Who we could see, smell, hear, touch and (through the Eucharist) taste! When we look upon a statue as we meditate in prayer to God, our senses are illuminated. We are not worshipping the wood, plaster, plastic or paint. The image, though, appeals to our sense of sight, aiding in our visualization and helping us to focus on the pure, consistent and holy life lived by that saint...like the Blessed Virgin Mary, for instance. Here's a few more things to keep in mind:

• Stained glass windows with images can work in the same way...but most people don't seem to have a problem with those, because "they're just pretty".

• Images were very important in the early times of our Church's history, especially when most of the faithful were illiterate, and could not read the word of God on their own. The images helped them recall instances and situations in the Word that they had heard about, but could not read on their own.

• We put framed pictures of loved ones on mantles and walls of our homes, but that doesn't mean that we worship them.

• If I hold my Bible during worship, and hold it close to my heart...am I worshipping the God who inspired and wrote it, or am I worshipping the leather, glue and paper?

• The weatherman uses a visual aid of maps when forecasting the weather, but couldn't he just tell us the facts and read the temperatures?

• Is a Children's picture Bible that includes animations and drawings throughout it, the worshipping of images? Those are images, too, just not 3-D.

• Catholics may pray *in front* of a statue, but *never to* a statue...that would be idolatry.

Finally, consider these last two thoughts regarding what the early Christians did:

"Previously God, who has neither a body nor a face, absolutely could not be represented by an image. But now that He has made Himself visible in the flesh and has lived with men, I can make an image of what I have seen of God...and contemplate the glory of the Lord, His face unveiled."
- St. John Damascene (749 AD)

"The early Church used statues and images as aids to devotion and as expressions of faith. One need only to visit the catacombs in Rome to see statues and frescoes representing not only Christ but also scenes from Scripture. When the Church emerged from the catacombs, it continued to decorate its houses of worship with statues, mosaics, frescoes, and oil paintings, all designed to increase a spirit of prayerfulness."
 -Albert Nevins, M.M.

(Based, in part, on *Unabridged Christianity*, by Fr. Mario Romero, Queenship Publishing)

SAINT BIOGRAPHIES

TABLE OF CONTENTS

ST. ANGELA MERICI

FEAST DAY: January 27

Patron Saint of ill and disabled people.

HOMETOWN: Lake Garda, Italy

BIO -
At the age of 15 St. Angela began receiving graces from God telling her she would inspire women and their vocation. At the age of 56 while traveling to the Holy City on a pilgrimage she went blind. Not letting this stop her from traveling to the Holy City St. Angela opened her heart to the Lord

and continued on the trip. While traveling home after the trip she regained her sight. St. Angela felt this was a message from God and allowed her to open her eyes more to the surroundings of her daily life and allowed her to open her heart to the will of God.

A point in her life came when the Pope asked her to lead a convent of nuns, she said no! St. Angela was so connected with the Holy Spirit she knew that God was calling her elsewhere. In the time era St. Angela lived, it was not customary for women to travel alone or teach. So when she opened her eyes to her town she was saddened to see how many young girls where going uneducated. St. Angela helped gather a group of nuns who traveled around the city and gathered the young girls to help educate them. It is very easy for us today to go about our lives and contribute to society. We should look to St. Angela as an example to not continue to live a life of closed eyes and blocked hearts but to open up to the call of God and rely on prayer to remain in tune with the Holy Spirit and will of God.

"I shall continue to be more alive than I was in this life, and I shall see you better and shall love more the good deeds which I shall see you doing continually, and I shall be able to help you more."

ST. AUGUSTINE

FEAST DAY: August 28

Patron Saint of Theologians.

HOMETOWN: Numidia, North Africa

BIO -
St. Augustine, born in November 354, did not always lead a saintly life. He spent most of his early life living a wild and sinful lifestyle. He was no stranger to parties or other such activities. Growing up with his mother as a devout Christian (and now a saint) he was schooled in Christian thought, but never really had faith. He bounced around from one philosophical idea pool to another, trying to find truth. Meanwhile, he continued his life the way it was, not wanting to give it up. This is best illustrated in his prayer from his book Confessions, "God give me chastity, but not yet."

After years of searching and even more years of prayer by his mother, St. Augustine finally saw the Truth of the Church and converted to Christianity. He would eventually sell off his property to give money to the poor. He became a monk, and eventually a bishop. The decision to follow Christ comes at a staggeringly high price: the total transformation of life. St. Augustine shows us that to really find Christ; one must abandon the old sinful ways and take on the new life as Christ has modeled. When you are trapped in your old ways, or need the strength to turn from the snares of this world, turn to St. Augustine for prayers of guidance.

"Our hearts were made for You, O Lord, and they are restless until they rest in you."

"Jesus Christ will be Lord of all, or he will not be Lord at all."

ST. BERNADETTE

FEAST DAY: April 16

Patron Saint of the sick and of
people ridiculed for their faith.

HOMETOWN: Lourdes, France

BIO -
Although it may not have appeared
so on the surface, St. Bernadette was
an incredibly blessed woman. Born in
1844 in Lourdes, France, she entered
the world in poverty. In order to help
the family financially, she was hired
out to another family as a servant at
age twelve and was there until she was

fourteen. When she was fourteen, she received the first of eighteen apparitions by the Blessed Virgin in Lourdes, France. After receiving the apparitions, she moved into a house of sisters who taught her to write, and cared for
her sick body. When she turned twenty-two she was admitted into the order.
She spent the majority of the rest of her life sick, and was not often treated
with respect by her superiors. She knew what it was like to be ridiculed for
her faith. At the time of her apparitions, it is safe to assume that not everyone
welcomed her with open arms. She endured the mockery of others for what
she had seen because she knew it to be true. When convicted in belief, nothing can stand in the way of faith. It is not easy to face scorn and ridicule when
you feel alone in your faith. It is wise to turn to St. Bernadette for prayers of
strength and comfort.

"The more I am crucified, the more I rejoice."

"Nothing is anything more to me; everything is nothing to me, but Jesus:
neither things nor persons, neither ideas nor emotions, neither honor nor
sufferings. Jesus is for me honor, delight, heart and soul."

ST. BRIDGET OF SWEDEN

FEAST DAY: July 23

Patron Saint of Europe.

HOMETOWN: Numidia, North Africa

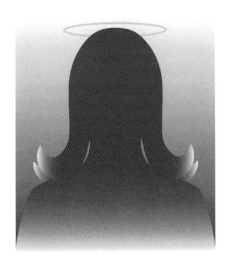

BIO -
St. Bridget was raised in a very afflu-ent household. She was the daughter of one of the most powerful gover-nors and landowners in Sweden. At the young age of fourteen, she was wed to Ulf Gunmarsson, a Swed-ish prince. Throughout her life she received various visions from God, directing her to act in a certain way or to tell some one something. Many of the visions she received asked her to reveal things that were highly unpopular in her court. Yet she remained faithful to the visions, even in the face of seri-ous harassment. After a pilgrimage with her husband, on which he fell ill and nearly died, the couple decided to enter the religious life separately to devote their entirety to God. While in the religious life, her visions continued and she founded many new convents to help bring people to the Lord. St. Bridget was fortunate, albeit blessed, in her life to have experienced "living for God" in many different ways. First she was a youth struggling to know God, then a wife, then a princess, and finally a religious. She followed God wherever He led her. She did not worry about the future and she simply trusted in God. When we find it difficult to entrust our futures to God, it is wise to follow the example and ask for the prayers of St. Bridget of Sweden.

ST. CATHERINE OF SIENA

FEAST DAY: April 29

Patron Saint of temptation.

HOMETOWN: Sienna, Italy

BIO -
St. Catherine of Sienna was born in
1347 and was no stranger to the idea
of temptation. From early childhood
she was tempted with things from
all areas of her life that went against
her relationship with God. As a child
she had consecrated herself and her
virginity to God, so when her parents tried to get her to marry, she

had to resist. Her friends too would ridicule her and tempt her to do things
against God. They would tell her that things were not really that bad and try
to justify their own sinful actions. St. Catherine, however, was not so easily
swayed. She resisted all of their temptations, clinging to the Lord for help. She
became a Third Order Dominican sister. She spent the remainder of her life as
a counselor for a couple different popes. She was also blessed with the marks
of Christ from the stigmata. She was quite the example for her family and her
peers. Similarly she is an example to the entire Church. The Church holds her
intercession most valuable, especially in the area of temptation and protection
against it. The individual members of the Church should look to her with the
same fervor for her prayers and guidance.

"Charity is the sweet and holy bond which links the soul with its Creator: it
binds God with man and man with God."

"Everything comes from love, all is ordained for the salvation of man, God
does nothing without this goal in mind."

ST. CECILIA

FEAST DAY: November 22

Patron Saint of music.

HOMETOWN: Rome, Italy

BIO -
St. Cecelia was born in Rome in 230.
From a very early age she vowed life
long virginity before God, a vow she
kept even through the marriage that
she was forced into by her parents.
She converted her husband to the
faith through her constant prayers.
He was later martyred. Soon after
her husband's death, she too was
martyred by beheading. She was known for her singing of the Divine Praises,
the Psalms, and other Scripture. Her prayers of intercession are so valued
because of how she prayed while she was still on earth. When she prayed she
worshipped God with everything she had: her thoughts, her words, her voice,
and her musical ability. She is one of the best models we have of what prayer
should become in life, total and primary. When we find ourselves struggling
in prayer, or want to go deeper, St. Cecilia should be a primary intercessor
and example.

ST. CLARE OF ASSISI

FEAST DAY: August 11

Patron Saint of the media.

HOMETOWN: Assisi, Italy

BIO -
St. Clare was born into what most would call a good life in 1194. She was the daughter of a count and countess of Assisi, Italy. When she was young she had the fortunate opportunity to hear St. Francis preaching in the streets of her village. From that time, she felt a strong urge to give up what she had and to follow the Lord through St. Francis' example. Her family would not allow her to do such a thing because they did not understand. So, when she was eighteen, she ran away from her mother's palace to join Francis, who gladly accepted her. She followed him and eventually set up her own order, the Order of the Poor Ladies, now known as the Poor Clares. Later on in her ministry, she would watch as her mother and sisters joined her order, giving up all they had to follow Christ as she had done.

St. Clare did something that not many people would do. She went against what her family, society, and the world told her "to be". She recognized that her call is not of this world, but of God. We are similarly called to recognize this utterly important fact. No matter how we are told to live, the only One we should live for is Christ. He alone is worthy, and St. Clare clearly knew this fact. Her intercession and aid will help anyone who needs help going against the world to follow the will of God.

"Go forth in peace, for you have followed the good road. Go forth without fear, for He who created you has made you holy, has always protected you, and loves you as a mother. Blessed be you, my God, for having created me."

ST. DOMINIC SAVIO

FEAST DAY: May 6

Patron Saint of young men, the wrongfully accused and juvenile delinquents.

HOMETOWN: Riva di Chieri, Italy

BIO -
St. Dominic Savio was born in Italy in 1842. As a child, he became very devout in his faith. When he was twelve, he entered a boy's school run by St. John Bosco. Under the saint's direction, Dominic became an example for the rest of his peers. The love he genuinely felt for each one of his classmates was apparent in all of his actions. He spent time each day praying for them and for mercy from their sins. There are multiple accounts when his classmates would be fighting and Dominic would intervene, tell them to look at what they were doing, and consider the Cross of Christ. Even in the face of harassment and ridicule, St. Dominic would continue to pray for them and help them through their sins. At age fifteen, St. Dominic contracted a terrible disease and died shortly after. Looking for help when it seems as if no one believes you, St. Dominic Savio's intercession can be precious.

"I am not capable of doing big things, but I want to do everything, even the smallest things, for the greater glory of God."

"Nothing seems tiresome or painful when you are working for a Master who pays well; who rewards even a cup of cold water given for love of Him."

ST. ELIZABETH OF HUNGARY

FEAST DAY: November 17

Patron Saint of Charities.

HOMETOWN: Presburg, Hungary

BIO -
Born of a king, and raised in a court,
the life of Elizabeth of Hungary
was far from wanting except for the
insatiable desire to do the will of God.
Though she was betrothed at the
age of four and married at the age of
fourteen, Elizabeth always showed a
great desire to follow in the path of
the saints and dedicate her life to the

poor. She built hospitals and shelters for the abundant poor that surrounded
her and made personal visits to them daily. On top of this she was a good
queen, a loving mother, and a dedicated wife. Elizabeth would be found many
nights in prayer vigils and fasting, never allowing these trials to interfere with
her life at court.

Though she only lived to the age of twenty four, Elizabeth of Hungary led a
life of piety, meekness, and charity and is a fantastic example of Christian
motherhood. She made the best of the graces that were given to her in life,
and always sought the good of God's people over that of herself. Even if such a
life might seem impossible for us, we should all look to St Elizabeth for guidance and assistance in the opportunities God puts in our life.

ST. FRANCES CABRINI

FEAST DAY: December 22

Patron Saint of immigrants and orphans.

HOMETOWN: Lombardy, Italy

BIO -
Frances Cabrini was one of thirteen children born in Lombardy, Italy and raised on a farm. She felt the calling to the religious life at a very early point in her life and, at the age of eighteen, attempted to take the veil. Unfortunately, poor health prevented her from being admitted and a priest friend asked that she instead teach at an orphanage for girls. After six years of teaching, she made a second attempt at the holy sisterhood and was successful. After taking her vows, her bishop requested that she start an order dedicated to the education and care of the poor children in hospitals and orphanages. Upon instruction of Pope Leo XIII, Frances moved her order, *The Missionary Sisters of the Sacred Heart*, to the United States. She spent much of her time assisting immigrants, especially Italians, and caring for the numerous orphans of New York City.

During her life, St Frances Cabrini founded 67 establishments including hospitals, orphanages, and schools. She was the first United States citizen to be canonized and is an intercessor for immigrants and orphans.

The example set by St Frances is that of simply heeding God's Will. She was told what to do, and she did it. It is true that the will of the God may seem hidden to us at times, but it is in these instances that we look to St Frances for guidance. If we were to quiet our hearts and trust in God's plan, He will reveal himself to us.

ST. FRANCIS DE SALES

FEAST DAY: January 24

Patron Saint of authors, confessors, deafness, journalists, educators.

HOMETOWN: Chateau of Thorens, Savoy, France

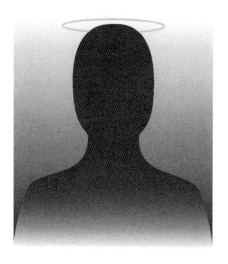

BIO -
St. Francis de Sales was born into a well-to-do family and his parents wanted him to become a lawyer, to enter politics, and to carry on the family line and power. He studied law in college, then finding a position as a Senate advocate. He then heard the message from God to "Leave all and follow Me" which Francis took as a call to priesthood. His family was severely opposed to this, but St. Francis' devotion to prayer and his gentle ways eventually won over his family. Later, he helped found the Order of the Visitation with St. Jeanne de Chantal and was named a Doctor of the Church.

St. Francis de Sales' patience with his family is a model for all who have difficult family lives. His patience and constant faithfulness to prayer and faith was his support as he dealt with his family in love. When encountering a difficult family member or family situations one would do well to remember the patience and love of St. Francis de Sales.

FEAST DAY: October 4

Patron Saint of animals and the environment.

HOMETOWN: Assisi, Italy

BIO -
St. Francis led a pretty rough life in his youth. Though born into wealth, he was known as a street fighter and a soldier. In one conflict during his military service, he was taken prisoner and held for over a year. During his captivity, he began to think more intently about God. When he was released he made a life changing decision to give up all his worldly possessions and to follow Christ. He began to dress in beggar's robes and beg to survive. He went around preaching the Gospels to everyone he encountered, spending great amounts of time caring for the sick and the needy.

As he preached, people began to follow him and eventually he started his own order, the Franciscans. He spent hours in solitude, praying in the wilderness and spending time with animals. He served his whole life in the same way, helping countless people in need. He loved what he did. Not everyone is called to live a stereotypical life; the key is to live for God, no matter what He calls you to do. When it seems as though life is materialistic, unfulfilling, or, even boring, St. Francis is the man to look toward for prayers and guidance; he knew what it meant to live for God, no matter what.

"Sanctify yourself and you will sanctify society."

"Start by doing what's necessary; then do what's possible; and suddenly you are doing the impossible."

ST. FRANCIS XAVIER

FEAST DAY: December 3

Patron Saint of Missions.

HOMETOWN: Uncertain

BIO -
St Francis Xavier led a life full of
adventure and excitement. From
his early youth he was dedicated to
preaching the Gospel and spreading the truth of Jesus. He was one of
the original members of the Society
of Jesus, an order established by St
Ignatius of Loyola with the purpose of
revitalizing the evangelization of the
Gospel. He began his ministry by teaching the poor and zealously attending
to the sick in the hospital in Venice. After many tedious attempts and failures,
Francis was able to begin on his true calling as a missionary. Through the ten
years of his missionary travels, Francis preached in India, the Philippines, and
finally Japan.

Though he only lived for ten years of ministry, Francis reached more countries and converted more people than anyone else at the time and is considered the greatest missionary since the Apostles. Francis led a life of patience,
humility, courage and zeal for the Faith and is a great saint to pray to when
faced with those tough situations in life, when we find it difficult to live our
faith. The example of Francis is one that calls us on to stand out to make a difference when we don't think we have the strength or the ability to do so.

ST. GEMMA GALGANI

FEAST DAY: April 11

Patron Saint of temptation and pharmacists.

HOMETOWN: Tuscany, Italy

BIO -
It seems as though St. Gemma Galgani faced more hardships in her life than most anyone would have to face in two. She was born into poverty in 1878 along with her seven brothers and sisters. At age seven, her mother died. Then at age eighteen her father died and left her to provide for and

to raise her brothers and sisters. Around the age of twenty St. Gemma began to grow ill. Tuberculosis set in on her spine, leaving it curved. She developed meningitis which left her deaf. Due to large boil like objects on her head, her hair fell out and eventually her limbs were paralyzed. Through her prayer to St. Gabriel Possenti, she was miraculously cured.

Later in life she tried to join a religious order but was denied, so she remained a laywoman after God's heart. Even though her life was full of pain and sorrows, and things did not always go the way that she planned, she remained open to the will of God. Her story is a testament to the reality that even though things in life may be beyond our control, they will never be out of the control of God.

"If I saw the gates of Hell open and I stood on the brink of the abyss, I should not despair, I should not lose hope of mercy, because I should trust in You, my God"

ST. IGNATIUS LOYOLA

FEAST DAY: July 31

Patron Saint of the Jesuits, retreats and Soldiers.

HOMETOWN: Guipuzcoa, Spain

BIO -
Born in 1491, the youngest of 12, St. Ignatius of Loyola was first a soldier. In battle, he was hit by a cannon-ball in the leg and spent months in recuperation. During this period, he read through several different books including the lives of the saints. It was in these months that St. Ignatius was

transformed. When he had recovered, he gave up the uniforms of a soldier and put on pilgrims robes, gave up the vow of fighting for country, and took a vow of chastity. For a year he lived in solitary inside a cave, trying to find what it means to live a Christian life. At age 37 he began studying theology in Barcelona and Paris, finally receiving his degree six years later. Soon Ignatius founded the Constitutions of the Society of Jesus, later to be called the Jesuits. His life is an inspiration to those people who are struggling in confidence in the knowledge of their faith. When it seems like you do not know enough to share your faith or maybe not even enough to follow Jesus, St. Ignatius can be an invaluable intercessor for you.

"If God causes you to suffer much, it is a sign that He has great designs for you, and that He certainly intends to make you a saint. And if you wish to become a great saint, entreat Him yourself to give you much opportunity for suffering; for there is no wood better to kindle the fire of holy love than the wood of the cross, which Christ used for His own great sacrifice of boundless charity."

ST. JEROME

FEAST DAY: September 30

Patron Saint of Sacred Scripture and Librarians.

HOMETOWN: Strido, Dalmatia

BIO -
St. Jerome was extremely intellectual and found great joy in reading and studying Church documents. He contributed many writings and teachings to the modern Catechism. Jerome fought against allegations about the Blessed Mother's Virginity and published entire books to save the dignity of our Holy Mother. St. Jerome also defended the veneration of martyrs and their relics. Jerome spent the majority of his life contemplating the Churches mysteries, and attempting to make himself pure enough to receive even but a fraction of these answers.

For all those who enjoy learning more about the faith, St. Jerome is truly an inspiration. He has helped interpret and clarify even the most difficult theological questions. Fighting for ones faith is a grace from the Holy Spirit, and St. Jerome is a wonderful model for this grace.

"If the Apostles and martyrs, while still living on earth, could pray for other men, how much more may they do it after their victories? Have they less power now that they are with Jesus Christ?"

ST. JESSICA

FEAST DAY: May 24

Patron Saint of ?

HOMETOWN: Uncertain

BIO -
St. Jessica knew what it meant to
serve the Lord. She accompanied
Jesus along with the apostles and
a number of other women as He
traveled. She provided for Jesus and
the apostles as they spread the word
of God. It was also said that later
on when King Herod had John the
Baptist beheaded she was the one

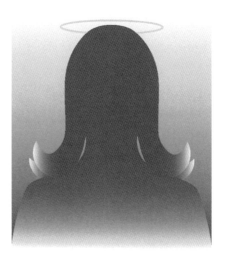

who went and gave him a proper burial in honor of the holy man he was.
She is also known for her service to Jesus, after He was laid in the tomb following His crucifixion she was one of the three along with Mary and Mary
Magdalene to return to the tomb to anoint the body; to much of their surprise
they were greeted by angels. St. Jessica shows that no matter how little something may seem, for God everything is a great service to Him and fills Him
with happiness. Pray to St. Jessica at times when you fail to serve or need help
serving the Lord. Also when you feel hopeless in service to God, know that
like St. Jessica everything counts.

STS. JOACHIM & ANNE

FEAST DAY: July 26

Patron Saints of parents and grandparents.

HOMETOWN: Nazareth

BIO -
Sts. Joachim and Anne lived very rich
and holy lives together. Unfortunately
for much of that time they were unable to have children despite their efforts. Finally in a last ditch effort they
turned to God. Humbly St. Joachim
presented himself in a temple on one
of the church's feast days. He came

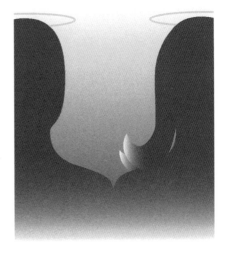

to offer his own life as a sacrifice to God because he felt unworthy as a man
being unable to provide his wife with a child. However at that time he became
overwhelmed, bowed in anguish and instead of returning home he secluded
himself in the mountain for a number of days. Knowing her husband's frustra-
tion, after he did not return home, she cried out to God asking Him that if
he would bless them with a child she would dedicate that child's life to the
service of God. Their prayers would be answered, "Anne, the Lord has looked
upon thy tears; thou shalt conceive and give birth and the fruit of thy womb
shall be blessed by all the world". Her husband received this same message
and returned to her at once. Soon Anne would give birth to Mary who would
become the Holy Mother.

Sts. Joachim and Anne shared such an immense love with each other. They
kept God right in the middle of their relationship and always tried to share
the love they had for God with one another. Their love for each other can be
an example we can use in our own families, relationships, friendships, and
even our special love shared with God. Pray to Sts. Joachim and Anne when
you are in need of guidance and when you struggle to love.

ST. JOAN OF ARC

FEAST DAY: May 30

Patron Saint of prisoners and victims.

HOMETOWN: Lorraine, France

BIO -
Born in 1412, St. Joan of Arc seemed to be destined for great things, even in her teenage years. At age 13, she began receiving visions of some of the saints and angels, including St. Michael the Archangel. At age 16, she saw a vision that told her to help Charles VII take the French throne from the English. Not exactly willing

to go to battle at age 16, she resisted the call for three years. Eventually she would go and lead the French troops into battle against the English. For more than a year she fought alongside her countrymen but was severely wounded. Her efforts were not in vain though; Charles VII took the throne in 1430. In the wake of her victory, she was captured and sold to the English who quickly put her on trial. Her trial would test her dearly, but in the end she would hold firmly the faith that brought her to that point.

For her beliefs and unwillingness to denounce her hope and faith in the Lord, she was convicted as a heretic and burned at the stake, a martyr. Most people will say that the courage and strength shown by this young saint only comes around once in a lifetime. Even more impressive is how St. Joan of Arc's story shows that through prayer and faith all will be given that same courage and strength. Her prayer can help you find that strength.

"About Jesus Christ and the Church, I simply know they're just one thing, and we shouldn't complicate the matter." (At her trial)

ST. JOHN BOSCO

FEAST DAY: January 31

Patron Saint of young people.

HOMETOWN: Piedmont, Italy

BIO -
In 1815 St. John Bosco was born in Italy. Two years later his father died, leaving his mother to provide for the family. When he reached a capable age, he began to do side work to earn extra money for his family. He would go to the circus near his house and observe the magicians doing their tricks, learn them, and then perform them for the boys around the neighborhood. After his one-man show, he would recite the homily that he had heard in Church the weekend before to all the boys. To put himself through college he worked a variety of odd jobs. He became a priest in 1841 and soon after, became a teacher. He had a passion to work with the youth, taking every opportunity to gather with them and teach them the Scriptures or catechism. Many of his writings were aimed at children and young adults to explain the faith to them.

He was a leader from his youth, standing in front of his peers, preaching the Gospel to them without reservation. St. John Bosco's intercession is perfect for anyone looking for an example of how to preach the Gospel to peers, or to anyone.

"All for God and for His Glory. In whatever you do, think of the Glory of God as your main goal."

"You can do nothing with children unless you win their confidence and love by bringing them into touch with yourself, by breaking through all the hindrances that keep them at a distance. We must accommodate ourselves to their tastes, we must make ourselves like them."

FEAST DAY: June 26

Patron Saint of ?

HOMETOWN: Barbasto, Spain

BIO -
St. Josemaria is one of the earlier saints of the 20th Century, born in 1902. At the age of 23 he was ordained a priest and began his ministry. Josemaria felt that God was calling him to a specific mission and in 1928 he founded Opus Dei; a devotion within the church to help all kinds of people to follow Christ and to grow in holiness. Opus Dei spread widely among countries and Josemaria suffered much persecution for its teachings. Although this was a very difficult time for St. Josemaria to stand by what he knew God wanted him to do, his perseverance allowed Opus Dei to spread the love of God to many places among many people.

If ever someone has felt that God was calling them to start something new, or help others to see His light in a different way, St. Josemaria Escriva is an excellent saint to ask for help. His faith in God's will was so great that he did not fall from what God asked him to do, even in the face of alienation from others. Do not be afraid of being shunned by peers while doing God's will, because it is Him that we must strive to please.

ST. JOSEPH OF CUPERTINO

FEAST DAY: September 18

Patron Saint of pilots, students, and test takers.

HOMETOWN: Cupertino

BIO -
St. Joseph of Cupertino was a difficult child; his mother often had to be
strict with him until Joseph overcame
the temper he had. He hardly had any
education and wasn't the smartest of
men. But regardless of the torment
he received he became very joyous
and loving as he grew up. Many saw
Joseph as a lost cause, he would accept this, and at age 17 went from friary to
friary, he was denied each time because he had no education, but he didn't
give up finally another friary accepted him as a lay-brother. He was given
many duties and jobs in the friary but Joseph would often forget about them
or mess them up. As a result of his mishaps, the monastery sent him away
because he was unsuitable for the work he needed to get done.

He continued to pray and finally a nearby Franciscan friary let him become an
oblate servant. Through his actions of joy and love the friars noticed his desire
to serve, and they accepted him into the order. He quickly became a deacon
but to become a priest he would have to be tested. The bishop before ordain-
ing Joseph asked him one question from a verse in the gospel of Luke. Luckily
for Joseph that one verse he knew out of the entire bible, Joseph was finally
ordained a priest. He would often receive deep visions through the sound of
a church bell, the sight of a holy picture, or even the thought of God among
many other things would bring him into such a vision. Nothing could snap
him out of these visions. During these it was common to see the Flying Friar
as he was known because he would levitate and often heard heavenly music. If
you ever feel nervous for a test or feel like you are a lost cause remember how
hard St. Joseph worked and pray to him for help.

"Clearly, what God wants above all is our will which we received as a free gift
from God in creation and possess as though our own."
- St. Joseph of Cupertino

ST. JUAN DIEGO

FEAST DAY: December 9

Patron Saint of ?

HOMETOWN:
Tlayacac, Cuauhtitlan (about 15
miles north of modern Mexico City,
Mexico)

BIO -
St. Juan Diego was born a free but
poor man. He became a farm worker,
field laborer, and a mat maker. He was
married, but he and his wife had no
children. St. Juan Deigo was born a
pagan, but even then was a mystical
and religious man. At the age of 50, Juan Diego converted to Christianity. His
wife eventually died before him. The Virgin Mary appeared to St. Juan Diego
at Guadalupe on December 9, 1531, where Our Lady appeared to him as Our
Lady of Guadalupe. The major sign Our Lady gave to Juan Diego was filling
his mantel with roses in the middle of winter, and when he released them
from his tilma (cloak), the image of Our Lady of Guadalupe was imprinted on
his tilma.

St. Juan Diego is a model of faith and perseverance. Time and time again, St.
Juan Diego went to his bishop for approval to build a church Our Lady had
asked of him, and time and time again, the bishop denied Juan Diego. Juan
Diego's faith never faltered and he continually went back to Our Lady to seek
the way to convince hearts.

FEAST DAY: October 28

Patron Saint of Patron of Desperate Cases.

HOMETOWN: Cupertino

BIO -
Ever been in a situation where all seems lost? Or ever felt forgotten or underappreciated? St. Jude Thaddeus would probably know exactly how you are feeling. As one of the original twelve Apostles, he followed Jesus throughout his whole ministry. After the death, resurrection, and ascension of Jesus, St. Jude continued to spread the Good News of Christ to distant lands; he also found time to write a Letter that became part of the New Testament. His life would end like the lives of so many Christians of the time; he was beaten to death, and then beheaded for his faith. This martyr bears the patronage of desperate cases because the early Church often confused Jude for Judas, and therefore did not seek the saint's intercession, devotion to him lacked and was a sort of lost cause. The Church today does not make this mistake, St. Jude's intercession is powerful for anyone feeling forgotten, lost, abandoned, or desperate.

BLESSED KATERI TEKAKWITHA

FEAST DAY: July 14

Patron of the environment and ecology.

HOMETOWN:
Auriesville (New York)

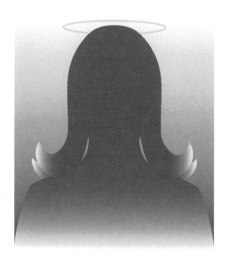

BIO -
Born in what would be today's New York state in 1656, Kateri Tekakwitha would become the first Native American to be suggested for canonization. The saint lost her parents when she was young to small pox, but came back strong. She met Father Jaques de Lamberville around 1675 and was brought into the Catholic faith the next year. After her conversion, she encountered staunch rejection and sometimes abuse from her relatives; they could not understand why she converted. Due to this abuse, she ran away to a Christian community that would accept her as she was. In her new home, she lived her faith to the fullest, even going so far as to take a vow of chastity at age 23. Even in the most difficult of situations, when everything seemed against her, Blessed Kateri Tekakwitha followed her heart to faith. She did not let any obstacle stand on her path to Jesus. When it seems as though you are stuck in your faith, people are ridiculing you for your beliefs, or you cannot overcome some wall in your journey, remember to ask Kateri Tekakwitha for her intercession.

FEAST DAY: March 3

Patron Saint of ?

HOMETOWN: Philadelphia, Pennsylvania

BIO -
Katherine Drexel was the daughter of a wealthy philanthropist and railroad entrepreneurs. She grew up with the strong example of faith and charity set by her parents which inspired her to follow in their footsteps. In an audience with Pope Leo XIII, she asked him to send more missionaries to Wyoming. The Pope replied "Why don't you become a missionary?" and Katherine did just that. She made her way out to the Dakotas where she spent millions of the family fortune aiding the Indians in that area. She eventually founded her own order *Sisters of the Blessed Sacrament.* She worked tirelessly for the spreading of the Gospel message. After a heart attack she had to retire from her physical work but never slackened in her prayer life.

St. Katherine lived a life full of generosity and kindness. We can all follow in her footsteps, even if not in the same way. Though we may get discouraged and think that we don't have the ability to do all the good that she accomplished, we must remember that St Katherine simply used what God had given her.

ST. LUCY

FEAST DAY: December 13

Patron Saint of those with hemorrhages and those with eye and throat
difficulties.

HOMETOWN: Syracuse, Sicily

BIO -
St. Lucy was born into a family which
was very holy. From an early age
Lucy knew she wanted to live her
life for Christ. Her mother arranged
a marriage for her; which Lucy was
very unsure about. She was able to
postpone the wedding for three years.

Until one day, Lucy was praying and miraculously her mother was cured from
her disease that caused her to have many hemorrhages and open wounds
covering her body.

In the face of rejection Lucy refused to marry, and as a result the governor
sentenced her to a life of prostitution. As the guards came to take her away,
they were unable to move her even after they attached her to oxen that attempted to pull Lucy. The governor became so angered her ordered for the
execution of Lucy. Lucy was tortured unmercifully; this consisted of having
her eyes torn out. They even tried burning her but yet again their greatest efforts weren't enough. As they were piling wood under Lucy the soldiers would
light the wood aflame and immediately it would be put out, causing no harm
to Lucy. Lucy was finally killed when she was stabbed preaching the Gospel
of Christ, but before she died her eyesight was restored which is the meaning behind her being the patron Saint of persons with eye troubles. Through
Lucy's example we can see that even in the face of rejection and persecution,
she still loved and served the Lord with everything she did. She also shows us
that you don't need to be able to see to believe. Pray to St. Lucy in times when
you can't see what God may be calling you to do in your life.

"Those whose Hearts are pure are Temples of the Holy Spirit." - St. Lucy

ST. MARIA GORETTI

FEAST DAY: July 6

Patron Saint of young women, chastity and rape victims.

HOMETOWN: Ancona, Italy

BIO -
St. Maria was born in 1890 into a family of six children. She was strong in her faith from the beginning, even in the face of great misfortune. At age six she lost her father to malaria. In order to survive, Maria and her family moved onto a farm of a nearby family. Six years later, at only twelve, she was attacked by the son of the farm-owning family. He attempted to rape her, but she fought vigorously against him, holding onto her faith the whole way. The man tried to choke her and then stabbed her fourteen times. She survived for two more days and finally took her last breath, clinging to a crucifix.

Before she died, she found the compassion to forgive the man for what he had done. While in prison, her attacker had a vision of Maria, adorned in lilies which she presented to him. Through this, he was converted to a life of faith. St. Maria Goretti is an inspiring example of chastity lived out in both word and deed. The Church looks to her for her intercession because of her faith, her ardent fight for what is right, and her selfless forgiveness of those who wronged her, even at such a young age.

FEAST DAY: April 25

Patron Saint of prisoners and lawyers.

HOMETOWN: Uncertain

BIO -
Author of the second Gospel, St. Mark was a part of the early Church from his childhood. His mother was involved as well, she often held meetings for the early Christians in her home. St. Mark was a disciple of Jesus and a traveling companion to Sts. Peter and Paul. He was a strong evangelist and founded many new churches. He wrote his Gospel account around 60 A.D. and it later became part of the official Canon of Scripture. St. Mark's outreach was phenomenal! He is a model example for a passionate proclamation of the life of Christ. His works are still reaching out to people, even thousands of years later! It makes sense that millions of Catholics have, are and will continue to seek the intercession of this saint. When you need help proclaiming the Word of God, St. Mark is your man.

ST. MARTIN DE PORRES

FEAST DAY: November 3

Patron Saint of African-Americans and innkeepers.

HOMETOWN: Lima, Peru

BIO -
St. Martin was born to a Spanish nobleman and a freed slave in 1500's. He spent his entire life in poverty, working with doctors and other people to make a living. It was here that he learned to care for the sick, a facet of his life that would eventually lead him to run an infirmary of the

Dominican order. He started as a servant and a beggar for the Dominicans, asking for money from the those people that were more fortunate financially to help care for the sick and poor. As head of the infirmary he was known for the great love and care with which he tended to the poor, as well as the miraculous healings that he worked in the name of Christ. He would later establish various orphanages as well as animal shelters to care for all of God's creatures.

Due to his great works, his Dominican superiors dropped the rule that no black man could become part of the order. St. Martin became a Dominican in 1603. Martin spent his life with those that most the world would look down upon. He humbly answered the call of the Lord to serve those who needed it most, and through this humility and steadfast faith, worked great wonders. No matter how cast out he felt, he would never shy away from his duty. He was a servant in poverty in his very being, and nothing could make him forfeit that. No matter who you are, St. Martin's prayers and life can help show that feeling unwelcome or left out is not necessary.

FEAST DAY: July 22

Patron Saint of converts.

HOMETOWN: Northern Galilee

BIO -
St. Mary Magdalene lived in the same time of Jesus. She began early in her life living a life of prostitution. Confused in many ways she sold her body as her profession, as an attempt to make money. Mary Magdalene didn't know the true love of God at that time in her life. She was constantly running from the law and getting in trouble. Finally one day she was caught by some officers and condemned to death by being stoned. As the pharasies and the towns people began throwing stones Jesus and his apostles heard the commotion and Jesus stepped in front of them demanding them to stop. Jesus called out those condemning Mary Magdalene saying, "If any of you is without sin, let him be the first to throw a stone at her" John 8: 7. They all dropped their stones and walked away. She was amazed at Jesus' love for her. From that point on she converted to a life full of love and service to God, and beginning then the only thing she could do was to love God the one who had saved her life and all our lives. She was also one of the three that returned to Jesus' tomb after his crucifixion only to encounter two angels and an empty tomb. Mary Magdalene showed us how, no matter how far we put ourselves from God, that He will always love us and provide us the opportunity to turn back to Him, as He did for her. She is an example of true conversion. We are all capable of loving and serving the Lord. Pray to her at times when you think you or someone else is distant from God and at times when you or someone you love is in need of a converted heart.

FEAST DAY: September 21

Patron Saint of money managers.

HOMETOWN: Uncertain

BIO -
St. Matthew lived a hard life, he was a tax collector, this was a very life, not many people liked him as he was the one who was taking all their money for the government. Most of these people didn't have very much money to begin with. Since the government did not pay him he would have to charge the people more money for himself so he could live.

One day Matthew was doing his job going from house to house, when Jesus confronted him and asked Matthew to lay down everything he had and to follow the will of God. With no questions asked Matthew did as he was told, put down everything and followed Jesus. Matthew's will to serve is something we can all look at as an example. Matthew humbly gave up his life to evangelize and is best known for being one of the four Gospel writers. Pray to St. Matthew when you may have hesitated and are nervous about God's own call for you.

"For I have not come to call the righteous, but sinner." - Matthew 9:13

ST. MAXIMILIAN KOLBE

FEAST DAY: August 14

Patron of Drug Abuse Victims.

HOMETOWN: Poland

BIO -
St. Maximilian Kolbe was born in 1894. He received a vision of the Blessed Virgin Mary as a young boy during which he was given a choice to become a martyr or a priest; he chose to become both. Maximilian became a Franciscan and founded the Immaculata Movement devoted to Our Lady. In 1941 Maximilian was arrested by the Nazi party and sent to the Auschwitz concentration camp. It was there that Maximilian Kolbe was murdered. He gave his life up for a young husband and father who was selected at random to die of starvation along with nine other men. Maximilian offered to take the man's place in the death chamber.

Anybody who has ever wanted the courage to help someone can relate to Maximilian Kolbe. He died for a man whom he had never met before. St. Maximilian Kolbe can give strength to those who desire the strength to save someone else. Maximilian's love for Our Mother Mary helped him to have the bravery and endurance needed to suffer physically, and yet never once turn from his faith.

"If angles could be jealous of men, they would be so for one reason: Holy Communion"

ST. MONICA

FEAST DAY: August 27

Patron of Wives and Abuse Victims.

HOMETOWN: North Africa

BIO -
St. Monica grew up in North Africa, at the time it was customary for women to have arranged marriages. St. Monica was arranged in a marriage to a Pagan Official of North Africa although he was a much older and generous man, he also had a temper and was violent. To make matters worse, St Monica's Mother-in-law lived with them, but the woman did not help St. Monica when she was being abused by her husband.

Through years of prayer and dedication to her faith St. Monica was able to raise three children Perpetua, Navigious, and Augustine, two of whom chose the Holy Life. St. Monica was also able to convert her husband and mother-in-law to the Catholic Church. At times raising her children was not easy. St. Monica consistently prayed for 17 years for her child Augustine to change his life to one of obedience to God. The priests would avoid her because her passion and persistence in prayer. St. Monica is a true example of dedication in prayer. Being bruised and broken, prayer was the first thing on her mind. At times it's hard but with consistence in prayer anything is possible.

ST. PATRICK

FEAST DAY: March 17

Patron Saint of Ireland and against snakes.

HOMETOWN: Kilpatrick, Scotland

BIO -

St. Patrick, born in 387, spent the first fourteen years of his life in Scotland. When he was fourteen, he was captured and taken to Ireland. At this time Ireland was a pagan nation that was far different than what Patrick had ever seen. While he was there he was forced into shepherding for six years. It was during his captivity that he would turn to God, praying daily, asking for strength to help see him through. He also used his enslavement to learn the language and customs of the people of Ireland. At age twenty he escaped his captors and fled back to his family. He continued to pray and to his surprise felt a strong call to return to Ireland and preach the Gospel.

He studied hard, became a priest, and set off for Ireland. He spent the remainder of his life in Ireland preaching and setting up churches wherever he went. For St. Patrick, it would have been easy to doubt that God had a plan for him while enslaved, but he stood firm in his faith through it all. In the end, it was evident that God had used his captivity to prepare him to evangelize the people of Ireland. If you feel that God is not present in your life, feel enslaved, or feel that God does not have a plan for your life, ask for the prayers of St. Patrick.

"If I am worthy, I am ready also to give up my life, without hesitation and most willingly, for Christ's name. I want to spend myself for that country, even in death, if the Lord should grant me this favor."

ST. PAUL

FEAST DAY: June 29

Patron Saint for Catholics for Truth.

HOMETOWN: Tarsus, Rome

BIO -
St. Paul was originally named Saul
and was a persecutor of the Christians. When St. Stephen became the
first Deacon to be martyred for his
faith, St. Paul was among the first
to throw a stone. On his journey to
Damascus to arrest more Christians,
God struck him with a bright light
and told him that when he was per-
secuting these Christians, he was persecuting Jesus as well. This is when Saul
was baptized and changed his name to Paul. St. Paul soon began missionary
work and converted many.

Are we persecuting Christ in the form of others in some way? St. Paul is an
amazing reminder that God lives within each person and His children must
love even the most difficult of people because God is present within their
heart as well. Even after Saul stoned and helped murder the first Deacon
martyr, the Holy Spirit still found a way to make him a tool of Christ and lead
thousands to Jesus. St. Paul is an incredible example of God's mercy, and
reminds us that everyone is capable of conversion and serving God in a new
way.

ST. PHILOMENA

FEAST DAY: ?

Patron Babies, Infants, and Youth.

HOMETOWN: Uncertain

BIO -
The story of St. Philomena holds an interesting tradition within the Church. Little to nothing is known about the life she lived while on this earth. It is known that during the early days of the Church, St. Philomena was martyred when she was only fourteen years old. Early in the nineteenth century, her remains were found covered by rocks that had markings on them indicating her name and the fact that she was martyred. Her remains are displayed in a chapel in Mugnano, Italy and many visitors have been blessed with joy, healings, and other miracles. Through these miracles and the private revelation of people, she was canonized by Pope Gregory XVI, making her the only saint to have been canonized solely based on miraculous intercession. It is obvious that there was something special about this fourteen year old girl. So young, yet she must have lived her faith vibrantly, even to the point of death. As the patron saint of the youth, she listens to the needs of those who pray for her help and answers them.

FEAST DAY: September 23

Patron of Civil Defense Volunteers.

HOMETOWN: Pietrelcina, Italy

BIO -
Born Francesco Forgione to a family of farmers in Italy, he joined the Capuchins at the age of 15. Taking the name Pio took the name Pio and was ordained in 1910. Eight years later Padre Pio began receiving many graces from the Holy Spirit. One day after Mass Padre Pio was kneeling before the Crucifix and Jesus appeared to him. It was then that Padre Pio became the first Catholic priest to ever bear the stigmata, which are the wounds of Christ. Padre Pio had the wounds on his hands, feet and side. It was even said that the blood from the wounds would smell of flowers. After the vision life became difficult, he was questioned if the wounds were real, and at times was not able to say Mass or hear confessions. At a later time he was able to continue his work.

After the daily 5-a.m. Mass Padre Pio would sit in confession for 10 hours at a time and would know the exact words to say to heal people's broken hearts. Padre Pio was even able to know if a person was holding back from a confession and would tell them what they needed to say as if he knew more about them than anyone else. The Holy Spirit allowed him to be in two places at once (bi-location) and to hold the Eucharist high at Mass for long periods of time. Looking at Padre Pio should be a joy, a man of such humility and passion for helping people heal their broken hearts and sicknesses. Padre Pio can help us in our daily lives to examine our conscience and help heal the broken.

"The life of a Christian is nothing but a perpetual struggle against self. There is no flowering of the soul to the beauty of its perfection except at the price of pain"

ST. RAPHAEL

FEAST DAY: September 29

Patron of Travelers, happy meetings.

HOMETOWN: Heaven

BIO -
St. Raphael is one of seven Archangels who are ready and willing to help any soul who desires their protection. God sent Raphael to help Tobias enter into marriage safely with a woman named Sarah. Raphael also comforted Sarah when she lost seven of her bride grooms on the eve of her weddings. Raphael means "God heals" and people have credited their healing to the aid of St. Raphael.
To help someone else in their time of need is a great blessing. St. Raphael did this when asked by God, and can help anyone who seeks his guidance.

ST. ROSE OF LIMA

FEAST DAY: August 30

Patron of Latin America and Philippines.

HOMETOWN: Lima, Peru

BIO -
St. Rose was originally named Isabel, but when she was a baby she was so beautiful that her mother named her Rose, and that named stayed with her. As St. Rose grew older she became more and more beautiful. She was so stunning that often people could not take their eyes off her. This frightened her because she did not want to cause someone else to lust after her and be in sin. So one day Rose rubbed pepper all over her face until it became blistered and red.

St. Rose is a wonderful model for any woman who has wished to be humble and love Jesus. Rose's love for Jesus was so great that it has been said when she talked of Him, her face glowed and her eyes sparkled. Jesus was the only man Rose desired to have a relationship with and refused to marry because her love for Jesus was so strong.

"Lord, increase my sufferings, and with them increase Your love in my heart."

ST. STEPHEN

FEAST DAY: August 3

Patron Saint of Deacons.

HOMETOWN: Uncertain

BIO -
According to the *Acts of the Apostles*,
St. Stephen was a follower of Jesus
Christ after the descent of the Spirit
at Pentecost. St. Stephen, "a man filled
with the Holy Spirit" (Acts 6:5) was
chosen along with six other men to
assist the apostles in their mission.
Tradition holds that these seven men
were the first deacons of the Church.

During his preaching, some people became jealous over the wisdom with
which he spoke, so they handed him over to the Sanhedrin. These people
even went so far as to present false evidence against Stephen, saying that
he was preaching that Jesus was to destroy the Sanhedrin and change the
Mosaic customs. Stephen gave his speech to the Jewish elders, never shying
away from his proclamation of the saving power of Jesus Christ, even in the
face of death. After his speech, he was found guilty, dragged into the streets
and stoned to death. As he was being stoned he cried out to heaven for the
forgiveness of his murderers.

Standing up for your faith is hard on a day to day basis, but when the pains of
death are added to the consequences of faith, only those with true faith can
stand. Allow St. Stephen's story and prayers be the strength needed to carry
out the Gospel, even in the midst of the hardest persecution.

"They threw him out of the city, and began to stone him. The witnesses laid
down their cloaks at the feet of a young man named Saul. As they were ston-
ing Stephen, he called out, 'Lord Jesus, receive my spirit.' Then he fell to his
knees and cried out in a loud voice, 'Lord, do not hold this sin against them';
and when he said this, he fell asleep." -Acts 7:58-60

ST. TERESA OF AVILA

FEAST DAY: October 15

Doctor of the Church, Patron Saint of sick people and loss of parents.

HOMETOWN: Avila, Spain

BIO -
St. Teresa of Avila was born in 1515. Growing up she was strong in her faith, studying the saints and pretending to be a nun. Early in life she contracted a disease that crippled her. In time and through faithful prayers to St. Joseph, she was cured of this ailment. When she was twelve, she lost her mother. In her mother's absence, she looked to the Blessed Virgin to be her mother. She felt strongly called to the religious life, but faced opposition to such a decision from her father. At age 17 she left her family and her home to enter a Carmelite house. Shortly after taking her vows, she again fell ill and never fully recovered.

As a nun, she thought that the house she was in did not meet proper standards, so she left it and founded a reformed convent with Saint John of Avila. As she went around founding new houses, she often faced harsh resistance from local authorities; however, she continued on her mission and never turned from God. Through all the pain she felt in her life, whether it is the loss of her mother or the physical illness that plagued her body. Faced with the opposition she felt from her father and others, she remained faithful and always strove to do the will of God. For all those people in pain, for all those who feel unsupported, and for all those who do not feel that they are strong enough to follow the will of the Lord, St. Teresa of Avila... Pray for us.

"There is no such thing as bad weather. All weather is good because it is God's."

"Dream that the more you struggle, the more you prove the love that you bear your God, and the more you will rejoice one day with your Beloved, in a happiness and rapture that can never end."

FEAST DAY: October 1

Patron Saint of missions, pilots, florists and AIDS sufferers.

HOMETOWN: Lisieux, France

BIO -
St. Therese of Lisieux was born in 1873 to a mother and father who were both incredibly pious people. She was raised with eight brothers and sisters. Her life was one continuous search for her proper vocation. She grew up in a uniquely devout household, watching several of her sisters enter

the religious life. Her mother died when St. Therese was only four, leaving her in the care of her father. The older she got, the less and less certain she became with regards to what she was being called to do. She felt a pull toward the religious life, but could not believe that she had what it takes to follow such a path. She never stopped praying for faith and strength to follow God's call, and her prayers were answered. When she was fifteen she asked the superior of a Carmelite house to allow her to take her vows. While, she was refused permission due to her age, she was not one to be turned away from God's will. She went to the bishop and when that too failed, she went bravely to the Pope who granted her admittance. God's plan for our lives is not always as clear as we would like it to be. Sometimes it may take years of discernment to figure out what God wants for us. Anytime you are feeling disheartened and on the brink of giving up, turn your eyes and prayers to St. Therese of Lisieux who knows exactly how you feel.

"You know well enough that Our Lord does not look so much at the greatness of our actions, nor even at their difficulty, but at the love with which we do them"

"Our Lord needs from us neither great deeds nor profound thoughts. Neither intelligence nor talents. He cherishes simplicity"

ST. THOMAS AQUINAS

FEAST DAY: January 28

Patron Saint of all Universities and Students.

HOMETOWN: Lombardy near Naples

BIO -
Probably one of the greatest Theologians of all time St. Thomas Aquinas was put into a Catholic School at a very young age. As a child in school the teachers were astonished at his intelligence and spiritual growth. When it was time for St. Thomas to decide what life he was going to live he chose the Holy Life. His family opposed his decision and tried everything to get him to leave the Holy Order of St. Dominic. They even sent him an impure woman to tempt him. With guidance from the Holy Spirit for strength he was not tempted, by being strong God gave him the gift of perfect chastity. St. Thomas went on to finish his Doctorate and continued to write prayers and books which are still used everyday all over the world. As teens praying with St. Thomas for the gift of chastity may help you receive strength in times of weakness and temptation. The only hope is to remain pure at heart and strong in prayer.

"We are like children, who stand in need of masters to enlighten us and direct us; and God has provided for this, by appointing his angels to be our teachers and guides"

"Charity is the forum, mover, mother and root of all virtues"

ST. THOMAS BECKET

FEAST DAY: December 29

Patron of Clergy, Exeter College of Oxford, Portsmouth England; Secular Clergy.

HOMETOWN: London

BIO -
Having an uneasy career St. Thomas was the Archdeacon of Canterbury England under the rule of King Henry II. At the age of 36 his friend King Henry II made him the Chancellor of England. Later when King Henry II felt it would be beneficial to him, he asked St. Thomas to be the Chancellor Archbishop of England. Hesitant to make the decision St. Thomas told the King that with his appointment there may be times when he would not agree with the King's thoughts or actions on the church.

A situation occurred when King Henry II tried to pass a constitution-allowing priests to be punished without trial. St. Thomas briefly signed the bill but realized his mistake and rejected the constitution fleeing to France fearing the wrath of King Henry II. He remained in France for 7 years in hiding. Knowing what King Henry II would do to him on his arrival back to London St. Thomas decided to go anyway. When he arrived back in London, King Henry II found out of his return and immediately sent 7 Knights to Canterbury Cathedral where he was killed. In our lives we should pray with St. Thomas to intercede for us to stand up for what is right even though there may not always be a positive outcome.

"The last temptation is the greatest treason: To do the right deed for the wrong reason"

ST. THOMAS MORE

FEAST DAY: June 22

Patron Saint of adopted children, politicians, and large families.

HOMETOWN: London, England

BIO -
When you think of a saint, you usually think of someone who dedicated their lives to poverty, chastity, humility and many of the other holy actions. St Thomas More is no different except that he did all this while living in the world and in the public eye. More began his life in fervent pursuit of

the religious vocation and was fully prepared to give himself to God entirely without reservation. Though this is a wonderful calling, St Thomas found that this was not for him and began his study of law.

More found success immediately and was soon given a position as an advisor to King Henry VIII, eventually moving all the way into the position as Chancellor of England. Here, Thomas faced his greatest trials when the king claimed to be the head of the Catholic Church in England. Thomas reacted to this by resigning from his post and taking on a life of seclusion with his wife and daughter. Though he was out of the King's court, he was never silent. He spent his days reading and writing in response to the actions of the king and his allocations against the Catholic Church. More was eventually arrested and sentence to death.

Thomas More is a saint that should be called upon whenever we find ourselves faced with trials or temptations and need the courage to stand up and be true Christians. He is also a great example of chaste Christian marriage and honesty, remaining always faithful and true to his wife even throughout his captivity.

ST. TIMOTHY

FEAST DAY: January 26

Patron Saint of internal pain, disease.

HOMETOWN: Perapa, Egyptian
Thebaid

BIO -
St. Timothy was born in Lystra
(modern day Turkey) sometime in the
first century. He was born of a Jewish
woman, but converted to Christianity
after hearing St. Paul preach during his first trip to Lystra. On Paul's
second visit seven years later, Timothy became close friends with him
and began to travel with Paul on his missionary trips. He would later be the
recipient of at least two of Paul's epistles found in the Bible today (1 Timothy
and 2 Timothy). Following the way of the Lord led Timothy to many different
regions. Tradition tells us that Timothy finally settled in Ephesus and became
their first bishop. It was there too that Timothy was stoned and clubbed to
death, thus placing him among the many martyrs of the Church.

In one of the letters of St. Paul, he urges Timothy, "Let no one have contempt
for your youth, but set an example for those who believe, in speech, conduct,
love, faith, and purity" (1 Tim. 4:12). It is this statement that has become very
encouraging for the younger members of the Church. Despite his young age,
Timothy found faith in the way of Jesus Christ and did not let anyone tell him
that he was too young to do great things for the Lord. So let all those who
seek to be heard but feel they are too young turn to the intercession of this
great saint.

ST. VICTORIA

FEAST DAY: December 23

Patron Saint of Cordoba Spain

HOMETOWN: Cordoba, Spain

BIO -
Although there is not much known about St. Victoria, what we do actually know is very inspiring. In the time she lived it was very customary for women to be arranged to marry complete strangers. St. Victoria was promised to a suitor but refused to marry him because of her love for Christ. Even when her suitor imprisoned and starved Victoria she persisted in refusing to marry him. Finally after years of trying to change Victoria's mind the man released her. Later Victoria refused to make sacrifices to pagan gods which was a popular custom in that time as well. Because she did not honor the pagan god St. Victoria was executed. A guard present at her execution was converted because of her faith, and he too was martyred.

St. Victoria reminds us that we must at all times act as a Catholic man or women. Even in her death she was able to convert a sinner because of her willingness to sacrifice her life for God. St. Victoria is a beautiful model of what it means to have faith in God's protection even when faced with death.

ST. ZITA

FEAST DAY: April 27

Patron of Servants.

HOMETOWN: Monte Sagrati, Italy

BIO -
St. Zita was born into a very poor, but
holy family. Her sister was a nun, and
her uncle was a hermit who was regarded as a saint by the town's people.
At the early age of twelve Zita started
working for a very rich family. She
was quickly disliked by her fellow em-
ployees because of the generous gifts
of her employers of food and clothing
to the poor. However the family could not ignore for long the presence of
God in this young girl. She eventually won the hearts of the entire family for
whom she worked.

Zita found time every day to attend Mass and prayed constantly to Jesus.
St. Zita is an amazing example to anyone who is being persecuted for doing
what is just in God's eyes. If anyone has every felt out casted by coworkers or
classmates for doing what is right, turn to St. Zita for strength to endure the
embarrassment. God took care of St. Zita through out her life, and promises
to do the same for anyone who acts out of love, especially when being persecuted.

RANDOM SAINT STORIES

Too often, I think, we associate saints with angels. Saints were not angels, and they were not perfect. Angels don't have human needs like saints did. Angels don't go to the bathroom like saints did.

Why am I bringing this up? Because we need to remember that what made the saints, well... saints was their response to God, through their humanity. The saints screwed up sometimes, the saints sinned sometimes, just like you and me. They fell down, but they got up again.

Below, I've assembled a list of some of the lesser known stories and quotes of saints. While some details are based on popular history and not public record, we must always be careful never to dismiss stories simply because they seem implausible. Never forget that all things are possible with God (Matthew 19:26, Luke 1:37). Some of these may strike you as pretty random, even fictional. There are thousands of more normal or less intriguing stories of our saintly brothers and sisters. It would be easy to focus just on those. The saints outlined here are no more or less important than others, and I hope we'll keep in perspective that this list of funny or "odd" stories is meant for reading enjoyment, not to make any statement about saintly spirituality. I've done this in hopes of reminding us that humor and laughter are just as essential to holiness as patience and piety. I hope this list makes you smile and laugh a little bit. Enjoy the lives of these saints... some might surprise you.

ST. JOHN VIANNEY
Ordained to the priesthood in 1815, St. John Vianney became a world-renowned priest (especially for his loving, simple and incredible demeanor in the Sacrament of Reconciliation). He was known for his very practical, "no-nonsense" attitude.

Once a visitor asked Father Vianney, "Father, why can we barely hear you when you pray, but when you preach, you practically shout?"

Father Vianney replied, "When I preach, I often am speaking to those who are deaf to the word, or those who have fallen asleep, but when I pray, I am speaking to God and I know that He's not deaf."

He was known to laugh, often, at himself, and his lack of talent in certain areas.

A professor once remarked (about St. John), "This fellow is a complete ass. What can he possibly accomplish?"

Father Vianney replied, "If Samson armed only with the jawbone of an ass, could kill one thousand Philistines, imagine what God can do with the complete ass!"

ST. MARY MAZZARELLO

Born into a very poor family and not very well educated, St. Mary Mazzarello spent a good deal of time ministering to the youth, especially girls, and eventually founded the Salesian Sisters.

Facing death, at the young age of only 44, St Mary Mazzarello was calm and cool. Just before she died she apparently remarked to a priest, "Well, that's the passport. I expect I can leave any time now."

POPE ST. PIUS X

Ordained as a priest in 1858, Giuseppe Sarto was elected Pope in 1903. He was a brilliant student and worked a great deal with the illiterate, undereducated and the sick and underprivileged.

During a religion class of the future Pope, the teacher told the class that he would give them two apples if anyone could tell him "where God is."

Giuseppe, later Pope Pius X, replied, "I'll give you two apples to anyone who can tell me where He isn't."

Many people found him so holy and impressive that they often regarded him as a living saint, to which Pius X replied, "Don't I already have enough to do? Now they want miracles, too?"

ST. JOHN OF BEVERLY

St. John was born in England, and eventually became the Bishop of York. He later founded a monastery at Beverly (hence, the title).

As the story goes, St. John of Beverly took youth on retreat once, in which one of the participants was a mute young man, who also happened to be balding. St. John apparently made the sign of the cross on the youth's tongue, who was then miraculously able to speak. Possibly just as incredible (to anyone who has lost their own hair) is that later the young man also grew back hair and was cured of his baldness... that is why St. John of Beverly is prayerfully invoked against baldness.

Wow, what a hairy situation, huh?

ST. AGATHA
Agatha was a noblewoman and a virgin from Sicily. In 251 a Roman Senator, Quintianus, made a physical advance towards her, which she quickly and loudly rejected. Enraged, he publicly accused her of being a Christian (illegal at the time) and ordered that her breasts be cut off. Through the intercession of St. Peter while she was imprisoned, however, they were restored. This is the reason that St. Agatha is the patron saint invoked against breast diseases.

They tried to kill her in a couple different ways that never seemed to work out. They attempted to burn Agatha at the stake (but she was protected), and a volcano erupted, interrupting the attempted murder. Later, they cut off her head.

ST. TERESA OF AVILA
Teresa grew up in a rich Spanish household, but became handicapped at a young age. After praying to St. Joseph, she was cured and went on to become a Carmelite nun with a strong devotion to Our Lady, the Blessed Virgin Mary. Later in life she had confirmed visions, was proclaimed a Doctor of the Church and became a mystical writer, dying in 1582.

Teresa found herself in several disastrous situations. Once after falling and injuring her leg, she looked up to Heaven and asked, "Lord, you couldn't have picked a worse time for this to happen...haven't I had enough problems?"

She said that the Lord replied, "Don't you realize that this is how I treat my friends?" St. Teresa of Avila retorted, "If this is how you treat your friends, it's no wonder you don't have very many."

St. Teresa was once recorded as saying, "A sad nun is a bad nun... I am more afraid of one unhappy sister than a crowd of evil spirits. What would happen if we hid what little sense of humor we had? Let each of us humbly use this to cheer others."

ST. MARK

Mark, one of the gospel writers, was a convert to Christianity. Though many mistakenly believe him to be one of the original twelve apostles, he was not. It was in his mother's home, that the early apostles met when in Jerusalem. He was later a traveling companion of Peter's, and most believe the young man who was present in the garden (and ran away naked) at the time of Jesus' arrest at Gethsemane.

It is said that once St. Mark was aroused by a beautiful woman who kissed his hand. He cut it off, only to have it restored later by the Blessed Virgin Mary.

Venice claims St. Mark as their own because he once sought refuge within its lagoons during a storm. An angel apparently appeared to the future saint telling him that "on this site a great city will arise in your honor." Years later, workmen were constructing St. Mark's Basilica near that same site. A workman accidentally fell from the steeple, yelling St. Mark's name on the way down. Miraculously, the falling worker was saved, when a tree branch appeared (out of the blue, and in front of witnesses) to support him before he hit the ground.

ST. CHRISTINA THE ASTONISHING

As a young girl, Christina suffered a "fit" (probably an epileptic seizure of an intense degree), which lead to a life of "paranormal" experiences for the holy young woman. Many of the weird occurrences were publicly and literally recorded by one of her contemporaries. She is the patron saint of psychiatrists.

It's historical record that at age 22, Christina died following a seizure. During her funeral Mass (in a crowded church) she sat up in her coffin in front of the entire congregation, and then flew up into the rafters of the church. The church emptied, leaving only her sister and the priest inside. After the priest convinced her to come down out of the rafters, she said that she was "repelled" by the smell of all of the sinners in attendance at her funeral. Later in life, she taught about how she had truly died and had even "seen" hell, and was depressed, seeing many of her friends there. She apparently also had a vision of purgatory, where she also saw friends, but was given the option of returning to earth. She opted to return in order to pray for those friends.

She grew old and was very well-renowned for her holiness and wisdom.

IGNATIUS OF LOYOLA
Founder of the Jesuits, Ignatius began as a soldier in the Spanish army, but was later converted and made it his mission to spread Christianity around the globe.

During the Inquisition, Ignatius was imprisoned for "teaching new ideas." He replied to his captors, "I didn't know that it was a new idea to teach Christians about Christ."

As the story goes, St. Ignatius was an avid pool player and quite good. One time a theologian bet him on a match. The wager was: if Ignatius lost then he would be the theologian's servant for a month, but if Ignatius won, than the theologian "would have to do one thing that would be to (his) advantage." St. Ignatius won, and the theologian spent the next month on retreat, performing St. Ignatius of Loyola's Spiritual Exercises.

BLESSED POPE JOHN XXIII
Pope John XXIII was born in Italy in 1881, and is known best for being the Pontiff who called the Second Vatican Council (Vatican II). He was ordained in 1904 at the age of 23, and was very well known for his incredible humility and sense of humor.

One time a new building was being built on Vatican grounds, and the architects sent the plans over to Pope John XXIII for his final approval. The Holy Father wrote the phrase, "non sumus angeli" atop the plans and sent them back. The only problem was that none of the architects spoke Latin. At once they had it translated, but were still puzzled as to what the Holy Father meant by His seemingly strange comment. Later, they discovered that the Pope had realized something that the architects had not...the plans did not include bathrooms.

Another time, as the story goes, a reporter asked the Pope, "How many people work in the Vatican?" Pope John XXIII replied, "About half."

- Mark Hart

THE DOCTORS OF THE CHURCH

ST. BASIL
- January 2

ST. GREGORY NAZIANZUS
- January 2

ST. HILARY OF POITIERS
- January 13

ST. FRANCIS DE SALES
- January 24

ST. THOMAS AQUINAS
- January 28

ST. PETER DAMIAN
- February 21

ST. CYRIL OF JERUSALEM
- March 18

ST. ISIDORE
- April 4

ST. ANSELM
- April 21

ST. CATHERINE OF SIENA
- April 29

ST. ATHANASIUS
- May 2

ST. BEDE, THE VENERABLE
- May 25

ST. EPHRAEM OF SYRIA
- June 9

ST. ANTHONY OF PADUA
- June 13

ST. CYRIL OF ALEXANDRIA
- June 27

ST. BONAVENTURE
- July 15

ST. LAWRENCE OF BRINDISI
- July 21

ST. PETER CHRYSOLOGUS
- July 30

ST. ALPHONSUS LIGUORI
- August 1

ST. BERNARD OF CLAIRVAUX
- August 20

ST. AUGUSTINE
- August 28

ST. GREGORY THE GREAT
- September 3

ST. JOHN CHRYSOSTOM
- September 13

ST. ROBERT BELLARMINE
- September 17

THE DOCTORS OF THE CHURCH

ST. JEROME
- September 30

ST. THERESE OF LISIEUX
- October 1

ST. TERESA OF AVILA
- October 15

ST. LEO THE GREAT
- November 10

ST. ALBERT
- November 15

ST. JOHN DAMASCENE
- December 4

ST. AMBROSE
- December 7

ST. JOHN OF THE CROSS
- December 14

ST. PETER CANISIUS
- December 21

INDEX OF PATRON SAINTS

Abuse victims
- Adelaide
- Agostina Pietrantoni
- Fabiola
- Germaine Cousin
- Godelieve
- Jeanne de Lestonnac
- Jeanne Marie de Maille
- Joaquina Vedruna de Mas
- Laura Vicuna
- Margaret the Barefooted
- Maria Bagnesi
- Monica
- Pharaildis
- Rita of Cascia

Academics
- Brigid of Ireland
- Catherine of Alexandria
- Nicholas of Myra
- Thomas Aquinas

Accountants
- Matthew the Apostle

Accused people, falsely
- Blandina
- Dominic de Guzman
- Dominic Savio
- Elizabeth of Hungary
- Elizabeth of Portugal
- Gerard Majella
- Helen of Skofde
- Margaret of Antioch
- Margaret of Cortona
- Marinus
- Matilda

- Menas
- Philip Howard
- Raymond Nonnatus
- Roch
- Serenus

Actors
- Genesius
- Vitus

Actresses
- Pelagia

Adopted children
- Clotilde
- Thomas More
- William of Rochester

Advertisers, advertising
- Bernadine of Siena

Against abortions
- Catherine of Sweden

Against battle
- Florian

Against bad weather
- Eurosia
- Medard

Against inflammatory diseases
- Benedict

Against perjury
- Felix of Nola
- Pancras

Against sorcery, witchcraft
- Benedict
- Columba of Rieti

Against throats ailments
- Andrew the Apostle
- Blaise
- Etheldreda
- Godelieve
- Ignatius of Antioch
- Lucy of Syracuse
- Swithbert

AIDS patients
- Aloysius Gonzaga
- Peregrine Laziosi
- Therese of Lisieux

Alcoholism
- John of God
- Martin of Tours
- Matthias the Apostle
- Monica
- Urban of Langres

Arm pain; pain in the arms
- Amalburga

Armies
- Maurice

Art
- Catherine of Bologna

Athletes
- Sebastian

Automobile drivers
- Christopher
- Elijah the Prophet
- Frances of Rome
- Sebastian of Aparicio

Bachelors
- Benedict Joseph Labre
- Benezet
- Boniface of Tarsus
- Caesarius of Nanzianzen
- Casimir of Poland
- Christopher
- Cuthman
- Epipodius
- Gerald of Aurillac
- Guy of Anderlecht
- John Rigby
- Joseph Moscati
- Luke the Apostle
- Marinus
- Pantaleon
- Roch
- Serenus
- Theobald

Baptism
- John the Baptist

Bi-racial or multi-racial people
- Martin of Porres

Bodily ills, sickness
- Alphais
- Alphonsa of India
- Angela Merici
- Angela Truszkowska
- Arthelais
- Bathild
- Bernadette of Lourdes
- Camillus of Lellis
- Catherine del Ricci
- Catherine of Siena
- Drogo
- Edel Quinn
- Elizabeth of the Trinity
- Gerard of Villamagna

- Germaine Cousin
- Gorgonia
- Hugh of Lincoln
- Isabella of France
- Jacinta Marto
- John of God
- Julia Billiart
- Julia Falconieri
- Juliana of Nicomedia
- Louis IX
- Louise de Marillac
- Lydwina of Schiedam
- Maria Bagnesi
- Maria Gabriella
- Maria Mazzarello
- Marie Rose Durocher
- Mary Ann de Paredes
- Mary Magdalen of Pazzi
- Michael the Archangel
- Our Lady of Lourdes
- Paula Frassinetti
- Peregrine Laziosi
- Philomena
- Rafka Al-Rayes
- Raphael the Archangel
- Romula
- Syncletica
- Teresa of Avila
- Teresa Valse Pantellini
- Terese of the Andes
- Therese of Lisieux

Bowel disorder
- Bonaventure

Boy Scouts
- Amand
- George

Breast disease, invoked against
- Agatha

Brides
- Adelaide
- Blaesilla
- Catherine of Genoa
- Clotilde
- Delphina
- Dorothy of Caesarea
- Dorothy of Montau
- Elizabeth of Hungary
- Elizabeth of Portugal
- Hedwig
- Ida of Herzfeld
- Ivetta of Huy
- Margaret the Barefooted
- Nicholas of Myra

Broadcasters
- Gabriel the Archangel

Broken bones
- Drogo
- Stanislaus Kostka

Cancer patients
- Aldegundis
- Ezekiel Moreno
- Giles
- James Salomone
- Peregrine Laziosi

Catechists
- Cesar de Bus
- Charles Borromeo
- Robert Bellarmine
- Viator

Catechumens
- Charles Borromeo
- Robert Bellarmine

Charities, charitable workers
- Elizabeth of Hungary
- Elizabeth of Portugal
- Vincent de Paul

Chastity, invoked for
- Agnes of Rome
- Thomas Aquinas

Child abuse victims
- Alodia
- Germaine Cousin
- Lufthild
- Nunilo

Children whose parents were not married
- Brigid of Ireland
- Eustochium of Padua
- Sibyllina Biscossi

Colleges, schools, universities
- Contardo Ferrini
- Infant Jesus of Prague
- Joseph Calasanz
- Thomas Aquinas

Comedians, comediennes
- Genesius
- Lawrence
- Vitus

Computers, computer technicians
- Isidore of Seville

Confessions, to make a good one
- Gerard Majella
- John Nepomucene

Cyclists
- La Madonna di Ghisalo

Dancers
- Genesius
- Philemon
- Vitus

Deaf people
- Cadoc of Llancarvan
- Drogo
- Francis de Sales
- Meriadoc
- Ouen

Demonic possessed people
- Amabilis
- Bruno
- Cyriacus
- Denis
- Dymphna
- Dionysius the Aeropagite
- Lucian
- Lucy Bufalari
- Marcian
- Margaret of Fontana
- Quirinus
- Ubaldus Baldassini

Desperate, forgotten, impossible or lost causes or situations
- Jude Thaddeus
- Gregory Thaumaturgus
- Philomena
- Rita of Cascia

Difficult marriages
- Castora Gabrielli
- Catherine of Genoa
- Dorothy of Montau
- Edward the Confessor
- Elizabeth of Portugal
- Fabiola
- Gengulphus
- Godelieve

- Gummarus
- Hedwig
- Helena
- Louis IX
- Margaret the Barefooted
- Marguerite d'Youville
- Monica
- Nicholas of Flue
- Olaf II
- Pharaildis
- Philip Howard
- Radegunde
- Rita of Cascia
- Theodore of Sykeon
- Thomas More
- Wilgefortis
- Zedislava Berka

Difficult situations
- Eustachius

Disabled or physically challenged people
- Alphais
- Angela Merici
- Gerard of Aurillac
- Germaine Cousin
- Giles
- Henry II
- Lutgardis
- Margaret of Castello
- Seraphina
- Servatus
- Servulus

Doubt
- Joseph
- Thomas the Apostle

Drug addiction
- Maximillian Kolbe

Dying alone; against solitary death
- Francis of Assisi

Dysfunctional families
- Eugene de Mazenod

Earaches
- Cornelius
- Polycarp of Smyrna

Elderly people
- Anthony of Padua

Engaged couples
- Ambrose Sansedoni of Siena
- Valentine

Ecologists, environmentalism
- Francis of Assisi
- Kateri Tekakwitha

Equestrians
- Anne
- George
- James the Greater
- Martin of Tours

Faith in the Blessed Sacrament
- Anthony of Padua

Fainting, faintness
- Urban of Langres
- Ursus of Ravenna
- Valentine

Families
- Adalbald of Ostrevant
- Adelaide
- Clotilde
- Dagobert II
- Dorothy of Montau
- Edwin

- Ferdinand III of Castille
- Ivetta of Huy
- Leonidas
- Leopold
- Louis IX
- Margaret of Scotland
- Matilda
- Nicholas of Flue
- Richard Gwyn
- Thomas More
- Vladimir

Fathers
- Joachim
- Joseph

Firefighters
- Barbara
- Catherine of Siena
- Eustachius
- Florian
- John of God

For help with conception
- Agatha
- Anne
- Anthony of Padua
- Casilda of Toledo
- Felicity
- Fiacre
- Francis of Paola
- Giles
- Henry II
- Margaret of Antioch
- Medard
- Philomena
- Rita of Cascia
- Theobald Roggeri

For people with mental illness, mental handicaps, and, against depression
- Amabilis
- Benedict Joseph Labre
- Bibiana
- Christina the Astonishing
- Drogo
- Dymphna
- Eustochium of Padua
- Fillan
- Giles
- Job
- Margaret of Cortona
- Maria Fortunata Viti
- Medard
- Michelina
- Osmund
- Raphaela
- Romanus of Condat
- Veran

Freedom
- Infant Jesus of Prague

Friendships
- John the Apostle

Gambling addiction
- Bernadine of Siena

Girl Scouts
- Agnes of Rome

Governors, rulers, authorities
- Ferdinand III of Castile

Grandparents
- Anne
- Joachim

Grooms
- Louis IX
- Nicholas of Myra

Guardian angels
- Raphael the Archangel

Happy marriages
- Valentine

Head injuries
- John Licci

Headaches
- Acacius
- Anastasius the Persian
- Bibiana
- Denis
- Dionysius the Aeropagite
- Gerard of Lunel
- Gereon
- Pancras
- Stephen the Martyr
- Teresa of Avila
- William Firmatus

Health
- Infant Jesus of Prague

Hemorraghes
- Lucy of Syracuse

Homeless people
- Benedict Joseph Labre
- Edwin
- Elizabeth of Hungary
- Lufthild
- Margaret of Corton

Homemakers, housewives
- Anne
- Martha

- Monica
- Zita

In-law problems
- Adelaide
- Elizabeth of Hungary
- Elizabeth Ann Seton
- Godelieve
- Helen of Skofde
- Jeanne de Chantal
- Jeanne Marie de Maille
- Ludmila
- Marguerite d'Youville
- Michelina
- Pulcheria

Incest victims
- Dymphna
- Laura Vicuna
- Winifred of Wales

Internet
- Isidore of Seville

Jealousy
- Elizabeth of Portugal

Journalists, news staff
- Francis de Sales
- Maximillian Kolbe
- Paul the Apostle

Knowledge
- Holy Spirit

Laborers
- Eligius
- Guy of Anderlecht
- Isidore the Farmer
- James the Greater
- John Bosco
- Joseph
- Lucy

Lay people, laity
- Frances of Rome
- Paul the Apostle

Learning
- Acca
- Ambrose of Milan
- Margaret of Scotland
- Nicholas Albergati
- Thomas Aquinas

Lectors
- Bede the Venerable
- Pollio
- Sabas

Liberal arts
- Catherine of Bologna

Loneliness
- Rita of Cascia

Longevity, long life
- Peter the Apostle

Loss of parents, mother, father
- Alphonsa of India
- Angela Merici
- Colette
- Dymphna
- Elizabeth of the Trinity
- Elizabeth Ann Seton
- Gemma Galgani
- Germaine Cousin
- Humbeline
- Jeanne de Chantal
- Jeanne Marie de Maille
- Kateri Tekawitha
- Laura Vicuna
- Louise de Marillac
- Margaret of Cortona
- Margaret Mary Alacoque

- Marguerite Bourgeous
- Marguerite d'Youville
- Maria Bagnesi
- Maria Fortunata Viti
- Maria Gabriella
- Maria Goretti
- Mariana of Quito
- Marie of the Incarnation
- Marie Rose Durocher
- Pulcheria
- Radegunde
- Rafka Al-Rayes
- Sibyllina Biscossi
- Syncletica
- Teresa of Avila
- Teresa Benedicta
- Therese of Lisieux

Lost keys, against losing keys
- Zita

Love
- Dwynwen
- Raphael the Archangel
- Valentine

Married couples
- Joseph

Mechanics
- Catherine of Alexandria

Migraine; against migraines; migraine sufferers
- Gereon
- Severus of Avranches
- Ubaldus Baldassini

Miscarriages
- Catherine of Siena
- Catherine of Sweden

Missionaries
- Francis Xavier
- Therese of Lisieux

Mothers
- Anne
- Gerard Majella
- Monica

Motherhood
- John Berchmans
- John Bosco
- Maria Goretti
- Pedro Calungsod
- Philomena
- Raphael the Archangel

Mountain climbers
- Bernard of Menthon

Musicians
- Benedict Biscop
- Cecilia
- Dunstan
- Genesius of Rome
- Gregory the Great
- Notkar Balbulus
- Paul the Apostle

Naval officers
- Francis of Paola

Newlyweds
- Dorothy of Caesarea
- Nicholas of Myra

Newborn babies, infants
- Brigid of Ireland
- Holy Innocents
- Nicholas of Tolentino
- Philip of Zell
- Philomena

- Raymond Nonnatus
- Zeno of Verona

Nightmares
- Raphael the Archangel

Nuns
- Ada
- Blessed Virgin Mary
- Brigid of Ireland
- Gertrude the Great
- Scholastica

Nurses
- Agatha
- Alexius
- Camillus of Lellis
- Catherine of Alexandria
- Catherine of Siena
- John of God
- Margaret of Antioch
- Raphael the Archangel

Newborn babies, infants
- Brigid of Ireland
- Holy Innocents
- Nicholas of Tolentino
- Philip of Zell
- Philomena
- Raymond Nonnatus
- Zeno of Verona

Obsession
- Quirinus

Opposition from Church authorities
- Elizabeth Ann Seton
- Joan of Arc
- Marguerite d'Youville
- Mary MacKillop
- Mary Magdalena Bentivoglio
- Rose Philippine Duchesne
- Teresa of Avila

Oversleeping
- Vitus

Pain, pain relief
- Madron

Parenthood
- Adelaide
- Clotilde
- Ferdinand III of Castille
- Louis IX
- Rita of Cascia

Peace
- Barnabas
- Elizabeth of Portugal
- Francis of Assisi
- Infant Jesus of Prague
- Irene
- Norbert

Penitent sinners
- Mary Magdalen

People
- Mary, Mother of God

Unattractive people
- Drogo
- Germaine Cousin

Physicians
- Cosmas
- Damian
- Luke the Apostle
- Pantaleon
- Raphael the Archangel

Pilots
- Joseph of Cupertino
- Our Lady of Loreto
- Therese of Lisieux

Poets
- Brigid of Ireland
- Cecilia
- Columba
- David

Police officers
- Michael the Archangel
- Sebastian

Poor people
- Anthony of Padua
- Ferdinand III of Castille
- Giles
- Lawrence
- Martin de Porres
- Nicholas of Myra
- Philomena
- Zoticus of Constantinople

Prisoners of war, pow's
- Leonard of Noblac
- Walter of Pontnoise

Priests
- John Mary Vianney
- Philomena

Pro-life movement
- Gerard Majella
- Maximillian Kolbe

Procrastination
- Expeditus

Prolonged suffering
- Lydwina of Schiedam

Radio
- Gabriel the Archangel

Rape victims
- Agatha
- Agnes of Rome
- Antonia Messina
- Dymphna
- Joan of Arc
- Maria Goretti
- Pierina Morosini
- Potamiaena
- Solange
- Zita

Retreats
- Ignatius of Loyola

Seminarians
- Charles Borromeo
- Lawrence

Separated spouses
- Edward the Confessor
- Gengulphus
- Gummarus
- Nicholas of Flue
- Philip Howard

Sexual temptation
- Angela of Foligno
- Catherine of Siena
- Margaret of Cortona
- Mary of Edessa
- Mary of Egypt
- Mary Magdalen
- Mary Magdalen of Pazzi
- Pelagia of Antioch

Silence
- John Nepomucene

Singers; vocalists
- Andrew the Apostle
- Cecilia
- Gregory the Great

Single laywomen
- Agatha
- Alodia
- Bibiana
- Emiliana
- Flora of Cordoba
- Gudule
- Julitta
- Margaret of Cortona
- Martha
- Nunilo
- Praxides
- Syncletica
- Tarsilla
- Zita

Skaters
- Lydwina of Schiedam

Skiers
- Bernard of Menthon

Slander
- John Nepomucene

Souls in purgatory
- Nicholas of Tolentino
- Odilo

Spasms
- John the Baptist

Speakers, lecturers
- John Chrysostom
- Justin Martyr

Spousal abuse; (physical)
- Rita of Cascia

Spousal abuse; (verbal)
- Anne Marie Taigi
- Godelieve
- Monica

Starving people
- Anthony of Padua

Storms, against thunderstorms
- Agrippina
- Barbara
- Catald
- Christopher
- Erasmus
- Florian
- Gratus of Aosta
- Henry of Upsalla
- Hermengild
- Jodocus
- Our Lady of Zapopan
- Scholastica
- Thomas Aquinas
- Urban of Langres
- Vitus
- Walburga

Students
- Albertus Magnus
- Ambrose of Milan
- Benedict
- Catherine of Alexandria
- Gabriel of the Sorrowful Mother
- Gregory the Great
- Isidore of Seville
- Jerome
- John Bosco
- Joseph Calasanz
- Joseph of Cupertino
- Lawrence
- Nicholas of Myra
- Osanna Andreasi
- Symphorian of Autun
- Thomas Aquinas
- Ursula

Swimmers, swimming
- Adjutor

Teachers, educators
- Catherine of Alexandria
- Francis de Sales
- Gregory the Great
- John Baptist de La Salle
- Ursula

Teenagers
- Aloyisius Gonzaga

Telephones
- Clare of Assisi
- Gabriel the Archangel

Television
- Clare of Assisi
- Gabriel the Archangel
- Martin de Porres

Temptations
- Angela of Foligno
- Benedict
- Catherine of Bologna
- Catherine of Genoa
- Catherine of Siena
- Columba of Rieti
- Cyriacus
- Elizabeth of Schonau
- Eustochium of Padua
- Gemma Galgani
- Helen del Cavalcanti
- Margaret of Cortona
- Maria Fortunata Viti
- Michael the Archangel
- Syncletica

Toothaches
- Apollonia
- Christopher
- Elizabeth of Hungary
- Ida of Nivelles

- Kea
- Medard
- Osmund

Traveling, finding lodging
  - Gertrude of Nivelles
  - Julian the Hospitaller

Unborn children
  - Gerard Majella
  - Joseph

Understanding
  - Holy Spirit

Unemployed people
  - Cajetan

Universal Church
  - Joseph
  - Peter the Apostle

Unmarried girls
  - Andrew the Apostle
  - Catherine of Alexandria
  - Nicholas of Myra

Vanity
  - Rose of Lima

Veterinarians; animal doctors
  - Blaise
  - Eligius
  - James the Greater

Virgins
  - Agnes of Rome
  - Blessed Virgin Mary

Virtue
  - Hallvard

Vocations
  - Alphonsus Maria de Liguori
  - Infant Jesus of Prague

Women
  - Margaret of Antioch
  - Mary Magalen

Women who wish to become
mothers
  - Andrew the Apostle

Women whose husbands are at war
  - Daniel of Padua

World Youth Day
  - Adolph Kolping
  - Albertus Magnus
  - Balthasar
  - Boniface
  - Caspar
  - Melchior
  - Teresa Benedicta of the Cross
  - Ursula

Young people
  - Aloysius Gonzaga
  - Gabriel of the Sorrowful
  - Stanislaus Kostka
  - Teresa of the Andes
  - Valentine

Zoos
  - Francis of Assisi

CALENDAR OF FEAST DAYS

FEAST DAYS IN JANUARY

1　Mary, Mother of God
2　St. Basil the Great
3　Most Holy Name of Jesus
4　St. Elizabeth Ann Seton
5　St. John Neumann
6　St. Gregory Nazianzen
7　St. Raymond of Penyafort
8　Blessed Angela of Foligno
9　St. Adrian of Canterbury
10　St. Gregory of Nyssa
11　Blessed William Carter
12　St. Marguerite Bourgeoys
13　St. Hilary
14　Servant of God John the Gardener
15　St. Paul the Hermit
16　St. Berard and Companions
17　St. Anthony of Egypt
18　St. Charles of Sezze
19　St. Fabian
20　St. Sebastian
21　St. Agnes
22　St. Vincent
23　Blessed Mother Marianne Cope
24　St. Francis de Sales
25　Conversion of St. Paul
26　Sts. Timothy and Titus
27　St. Angela Merici
28　St. Thomas Aquinas
29　Servant of God Brother Juniper
30　St. Hyacintha of Mariscotti
31　St. John Bosco

FEAST DAYS IN FEBRUARY

1　St. Ansgar
2　Presentation of the Lord
3　St. Blase
4　St. Joseph of Leonissa
5　St. Agatha
6　St. Paul Miki and Companions
7　St. Colette
8　St. Josephine Bakhita
9　St. Jerome Emiliani
10　St. Scholastica
11　Our Lady of Lourdes
12　St. Apollonia
13　St. Giles Mary of St. Joseph
14　Sts. Cyril and Methodius
15　St. Claude la Colombière
16　St. Gilbert of Sempringham
17　Seven Founders of the Order of Servites
18　Blessed John of Fiesole
19　St. Conrad of Piacenza
20　Blessed Jacinta and Francisco Marto
21　St. Peter Damian
22　Chair of Peter the Apostle
23　St. Polycarp
24　Blessed Luke Belludi
25　Blessed Sebastian of Aparicio
26　St. Porphyry of Gaza
27　St. Gabriel of Our Lady of Sorrows
28　Blessed Daniel Brottier

FEAST DAYS IN MARCH

1　St. David of Wales
2　St. Agnes of Bohemia

3 St. Katharine Drexel
4 St. Casimir
5 St. John Joseph of the Cross
6 Servant of God Sylvester of Assisi
7 Sts. Perpetua and Felicity
8 St. John of God
9 St. Frances of Rome
10 St. Dominic Savio
11 St. John Ogilvie
12 Blessed Angela Salawa
13 St. Leander of Seville
14 St. Maximilian
15 St. Louise de Marillac
16 St. Clement Mary Hofbauer
17 St. Patrick
18 St. Cyril of Jerusalem
19 St. Joseph
20 St. Salvator of Horta
21 Blessed John of Parma
22 St. Nicholas Owen
23 St. Turibius of Mogrovejo
24 St. Catherine of Genoa
25 Annunciation of the Lord
26 Blessed Didacus of Cadiz
27 Blessed Francis Faà di Bruno
28 St. Hesychius of Jerusalem
29 Blessed Ludovico of Casoria
30 St. Peter Regalado
31 St. Stephen of Mar Saba

FEAST DAYS IN APRIL

1 St. Hugh of Grenoble
2 St. Francis of Paola
3 St. Benedict the African
4 St. Isidore of Seville
5 St. Vincent Ferrer
6 St. Crescentia Hoess
7 St. John Baptist de la Salle
8 St. Julie Billiart
9 St. Casilda

10 St. Magdalen of Canossa
11 St. Stanislaus
12 St. Teresa of Los Andes
13 St. Martin I
14 Blessed Peter Gonzalez
15 Blessed Caesar de Bus
16 St. Bernadette Soubirous
17 St. Benedict Joseph Labre
18 Blessed James Oldo
19 Blessed Luchesio and Buonadonna
20 St. Conrad of Parzham
21 St. Anselm
22 St. Adalbert of Prague
23 St. George
24 St. Fidelis of Sigmaringen
25 St. Mark
26 St. Pedro de San José Betancur
27 St. Louis Mary de Montfort
28 St. Peter Chanel
29 St. Catherine of Siena
30 St. Pius V

FEAST DAYS IN MAY

1 St. Joseph the Worker
2 St. Athanasius
3 Sts. Philip and James
4 Blessed Michael Giedroyc
5 St. Hilary of Arles
6 Sts. Marian and James
7 Blessed Rose Venerini
8 St. Peter of Tarentaise
9 St. Catharine of Bologna
10 Blessed Damien of Molokai
11 St. Ignatius of Laconi
12 Sts. Nereus and Achilleus
13 Our Lady of Fatima
14 St. Matthias
15 St. Isidore the Farmer
16 St. Margaret of Cortona
17 St. Paschal Baylon

18 St. John I
19 St. Theophilus of Corte
20 St. Bernardine of Siena
21 St. Cristóbal Magallanes and
    Companions
22 St. Rita of Cascia
23 St. Felix of Cantalice
24 St. Mary Magdalene de Pazzi
25 St. Bede the Venerable
26 St. Philip Neri
27 St. Augustine of Canterbury
28 St. Mary Ann of Jesus of Paredes
29 St. Madeleine Sophie Barat
30 St. Gregory VII
31 Visitation

FEAST DAYS IN JUNE

1   St. Justin
2   Sts. Marcellinus and Peter
3   Blessed John XXIII
4   Charles Lwanga & Companions
5   St. Boniface
6   St. Norbert
7   Servant of God Joseph Perez
8   St. William of York
9   St. Ephrem
10 Blessed Joachima
11 St. Barnabas
12 Blessed Jolenta (Yolanda) of
    Poland
13 St. Anthony of Padua
14 St. Albert Chmielowski
15 Servant of God Orlando Catanii
16 St. John Francis Regis
17 St. Joseph Cafasso
18 Venerable Matt Talbot
19 St. Romuald
20 St. Paulinus of Nola
21 St. Aloysius Gonzaga
22 St. Thomas More
23 St. John Fisher

24 Birth of John the Baptist
25 Blessed Jutta of Thuringia
26 Blessed Raymond Lull
27 St. Cyril of Alexandria
28 St. Irenaeus
29 Sts. Peter and Paul
30 First Martyrs of the Church
    of Rome

FEAST DAYS IN JULY

1   Blessed Junipero Serra
2   St. Oliver Plunkett
3   St. Thomas the Apostle
4   St. Elizabeth of Portugal
5   St. Anthony Zaccaria
6   St. Maria Goretti
7   Blessed Emmanuel Ruiz &
    Companions
8   St. Gregory Grassi &
    Companions
9   St. Augustine Zhao Rong &
    Companions
10 St. Veronica Giuliani
11 St. Benedict
12 Sts. John Jones and John Wall
13 St. Henry
14 Blessed Kateri Tekakwitha
15 St. Bonaventure
16 Our Lady of Mount Carmel
17 St. Francis Solano
18 Blessed Angeline of Marsciano
19 Servant of God Francis Garces &
    Companions
20 St. Apollinaris
21 St. Lawrence of Brindisi
22 St. Mary Magdalene
23 St. Bridget
24 St. Sharbel Makhlouf
25 St. James the Greater
26 Sts. Joachim and Ann
27 Blessed Antonio Lucci

28 St. Leopold Mandic
29 St. Martha
30 St. Peter Chrysologus
31 St. Ignatius of Loyola

FEAST DAYS IN AUGUST

1   St. Alphonsus Liguori
2   St. Eusebius of Vercelli
3   St. Peter Julian Eymard
4   St. John Vianney
5   Dedication of St. Mary Major Basilica
6   Transfiguration of the Lord
7   St. Cajetan
8   St. Dominic
9   St. Teresa Benedicta of the Cross (Edith Stein)
10 St. Lawrence
11 St. Clare
12 St. Louis of Toulouse
13 Sts. Pontian and Hippolytus
14 St. Maximilian Mary Kolbe
15 Assumption of Mary
16 St. Stephen of Hungary
17 St. Joan of the Cross
18 St. Jane Frances de Chantal
19 St. John Eudes
20 St. Bernard of Clairvaux
21 St. Pius X
22 Queenship of Mary
23 St. Rose of Lima
24 St. Bartholomew
25 St. Louis of France
26 St. Joseph Calasanz
27 St. Monica
28 St. Augustine
29 Beheading of John the Baptist
30 Blessed Jeanne Jugan
31 Sts. Joseph of Arimathea & Nicodemus

FEAST DAYS IN SEPTEMBER

1   St. Giles
2   Blessed John Francis Burté & Companions
3   St. Gregory the Great
4   St. Rose of Viterbo
5   Blessed Mother Teresa of Calcutta
6   Blessed Claudio Granzotto
7   Blessed Frederick Ozanam
8   Birth of Mary
9   St. Peter Claver
10 St. Thomas of Villanova
11 St. Cyprian
12 Holy Name of Mary
13 St. John Chrysostom
14 Triumph of the Cross
15 Our Lady of Sorrows
16 St. Cornelius
17 St. Robert Bellarmine
18 St. Joseph of Cupertino
19 St. Januarius
20 Andrew Kim Taegon, Paul Chong Hasang & Companions
21 St. Matthew
22 St. Lawrence Ruiz & Companions
23 St. Padre Pio da Pietrelcina
24 St. Pacifico of San Severino
25 St. Elzear & Blessed Delphina
26 Sts. Cosmas & Damian
27 St. Vincent de Paul
28 St. Wenceslaus
29 Michael, Gabriel & Raphael
30 St. Jerome

FEAST DAYS IN OCTOBER

1   St. Thérèse of Lisieux
2   Feast of the Guardian Angels
3   Blessed Francis Xavier Seelos

4 St. Francis of Assisi
5 St. Faustina
6 St. Bruno
7 Our Lady of the Rosary
8 St. John Leonardi
9 St. Denis & Companions
10 St. Francis Borgia
11 Blessed Angela Truszkowska
12 St. Seraphin of Montegranaro
13 St. Margaret Mary Alacoque
14 St. Callistus I
15 St. Teresa of Avila
16 St. Marguerite d'Youville
17 St. Ignatius of Antioch
18 St. Luke
19 St. Isaac Jogues, John de Brébeuf
   & Companions
20 St. Maria Bertilla Boscardin
21 St. Hilarion
22 St. Peter of Alcantara
23 St. John of Capistrano
24 St. Anthony Claret
25 Blessed Antônio de Sant'Anna
   Galvão
26 Blessed Contardo Ferrini
27 Blessed Bartholomew of Vicenza
28 Sts. Simon & Jude
29 St. Narcissus of Jerusalem
30 St. Alphonsus Rodriguez
31 St. Wolfgang of Regensburg

FEAST DAYS IN NOVEMBER

1 Feast of All Saints
2 Feast of All Souls
3 St. Martin de Porres
4 St. Charles Borromeo
5 Venerable Solanus Casey
6 St. Nicholas Tavelic &
   Companions
7 St. Didacus
8 Blessed John Duns Scotus

9 Dedication of St. John Lateran
10 St. Leo the Great
11 St. Martin of Tours
12 St. Josaphat
13 St. Frances Xavier Cabrini
14 St. Gertrude
15 St. Albert the Great
16 St. Margaret of Scotland
17 St. Elizabeth of Hungary
18 Dedication of St. Peter & Paul
19 St. Agnes of Assisi
20 St. Rose Philippine Duchesne
21 Feast of the Presentation of Mary
22 St. Cecilia
23 Blessed Miguel Agustín Pro
24 St. Andrew Dung-Lac &
   Companions
25 St. Columban
26 St. Catherine of Alexandria
27 St. Francesco Antonio Fasani
28 St. James of the Marche
29 Servant of God John of Monte
   Corvino
30 St. Andrew

FEAST DAYS IN DECEMBER

1 Blessed John of Vercelli
2 Blessed Rafal Chylinski
3 St. Francis Xavier
4 St. John Damascene
5 St. Sabas
6 St. Nicholas
7 St. Ambrose
8 Feast of the Immaculate
   Conception
9 St. Juan Diego
10 Blessed Adolph Kolping
11 St. Damasus I
12 Our Lady of Guadalupe
13 St. Lucy
14 St. John of the Cross

15   Blessed Mary Frances Schervier
16   Blessed Honoratus Kozminski
17   Lazarus
18   Blessed Anthony Grassi
19   Blessed Pope Urban V
20   St. Dominic of Silos
21   St. Peter Canisius
22   Blessed Jacopone da Todi
23   St. John of Kanty
24   Christmas at Greccio
25   Christmas Day
26   St. Stephen
27   St. John the Apostle
28   Feast of the Holy Innocents
29   St. Thomas Becket
30   St. Egwin
31   St. Sylvester I